S0-BWE-035

THE STUDY OF THE LUGBARA:
EXPECTATION AND PARADOX
IN ANTHROPOLOGICAL RESEARCH

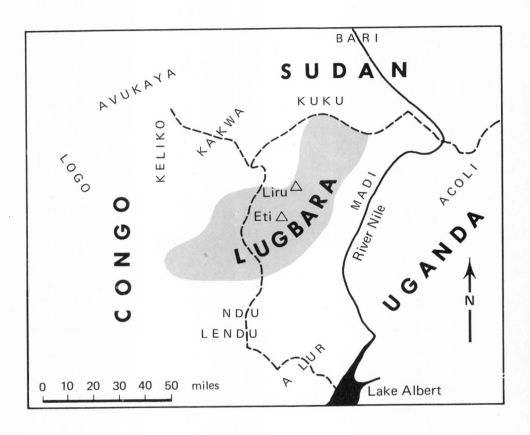

SUDAN

BARI

AVUKAYA

KUKU

KELIKO

KAIKWA

LOGO

Liru △

Eti △

LUGBARA

MADI

River Nile

ACOLI

CONGO

UGANDA

N

NDU

LENDU

ALUR

Lake Albert

0   10   20   30   40   50   miles

THE STUDY
OF THE LUGBARA:
EXPECTATION AND PARADOX
IN ANTHROPOLOGICAL RESEARCH

JOHN MIDDLETON
New York University

HOLT, RINEHART AND WINSTON
New York   Chicago   San Francisco   Atlanta
Dallas   Montreal   Toronto   London   Sydney

Copyright © 1970 by Holt, Rinehart and Winston, Inc.
All rights reserved
Library of Congress Catalog Card Number: 72–110498
SBN: 03–083985–8
Printed in the United States of America
1 2 3 4 5 6 7 8 9

for KIM

FOREWORD

Anthropology has been, since the turn of the century, a significant influence shaping Western thought. It has brought into proper perspective the position of our culture as one of many and has challenged universalistic and absolutistic assumptions and beliefs about the proper condition of man. Anthropology has been able to make this contribution mainly through its descriptive analyses of non-Western ways of life. Only in the last decades of its comparatively short existence as a science have anthropologists developed systematic theories about human behavior in its transcultural dimensions, and only very recently have anthropological techniques of data collection and analysis become explicit and in some instances replicable.

Teachers of anthropology have been handicapped by the lack of clear, authoritative statements of how anthropologists collect and analyze relevant data. The results of fieldwork are available in the ethnographies and they can be used to demonstrate cultural diversity and integration, social control, religious behavior, marriage customs, and the like, but clear, systematic statements about how the facts are gathered and interpreted are rare in the literature readily available to students. Without this information the alert reader of anthropological literature is left uninformed about the process of our science, knowing only the results. This is an unsatisfying state of affairs for both the student and the instructor.

This series is designed to help solve this problem. Each study in the series focuses upon manageable dimensions of modern anthropological methodology. Each one demonstrates significant aspects of the processes of gathering, ordering, and interpreting data. Some are highly selected dimensions of methodology. Others are concerned with the whole range of experience involved in studying a total society. These studies are written by professional anthropologists who have done fieldwork and have made significant contributions to the science of man and his works. In them the authors explain how they go about this work, and to what end. We think they will be helpful to students who want to know what processes of inquiry and ordering stand behind the formal, published results of anthropology.

ABOUT THE AUTHOR

John Middleton took his B.A. degree in English at the University of London in 1941 (he hoped originally to become an architect). After five years in the British Army, of which four were spent in East Africa where he was concerned mainly with African education and where he first learned that there was such a thing as anthropology, he returned to England and took his B.Sc. in social anthropology at Oxford University in 1949. He then spent two years among the Lugbara; he wrote up his field data as a dissertation and was given his D.Phil. in 1953. From 1953 until 1963 he taught at University College, University of London, except for two years which he spent at the University of Cape Town and Rhodes University (1954–1956) and a research trip to Zanzibar in 1958. After doing research in Lagos, Nigeria, in 1963–1964, he became Professor of Anthropology at Northwestern University. In 1966 he was appointed Chairman of the Department of Anthropology at New York University, where he has become particularly interested in the anthropology of urban-centered societies, which he sees as a main area for modern social anthropological research and thinking.

He has published several books, including *Lugbara Religion* (1960), *Land Tenure in Zanzibar* (1961), *The Lugbara of Uganda* (1965), *The Kikuyu and Kamba of Kenya* (with G. Kershaw, 1965), and *Zanzibar: Its Society and Its Politics* (with J. Campbell, 1965). He has also edited several books and published papers, mainly on the Lugbara. He is at present working on books on Lugbara politics and on the history of anthropology.

John Middleton lives in New York; he is married and has two children.

ABOUT THE BOOK

What does being a participant-observer mean? How can an anthropologist remain objective and at the same time become friends with the people he is studying? Should the anthropologist ever directly intervene in the course of events during his fieldwork? How can an anthropologist govern his relationships with various and potentially conflicting groups? When and how does the anthropologist cease being an outsider and become a person? What does one really do in fieldwork from day to day?

These are the kinds of questions that are asked about anthropological fieldwork. They are directed at that area of behavior that distinguishes anthropological research from that done by sociologists, psychologists, or representatives of any other behavioral science—unless they are modeling their field of behavior after that of the anthropologist. Participant observation as the *sine qua non* of anthropological field research becomes meaningful in John Middleton's terse, unpretentious, and thoroughly honest description of how he acted and felt as he studied the Lugbara—and while they studied him. Further, by stating what he thought at various times he was finding out, as compared to what he actually did discover, he gives the reader a thought-provoking introduction to the relationships between concepts, data, and interpretation. The realities of Lugbara life, as he discovered them through many months of direct experience, observation, and questioning, guide and check at every turn both the procedures of discovery and interpretation of what he did discover.

This study should be useful to any student who wants to do fieldwork in any kind of human community. Particularly in conjunction with the case study *The Lugbara of Uganda*, this volume should be useful in Introductory Anthropology courses. New students of anthropology are understandably curious about how the knowledge that makes writing an ethnography possible is gained, but anyone interested in the human side of human behavior and how it may be explored will find *The Study of the Lugbara* of compelling interest.

GEORGE AND LOUISE SPINDLER
General Editors
Stanford, Calif., January 1970

CONTENTS

THE STUDY OF THE LUGBARA:
EXPECTATION AND PARADOX
IN ANTHROPOLOGICAL RESEARCH

The ethnographer taking notes. The man in the center looking to his right is my guide Oraa. We were visiting a government chief and so were all dressed in our best clothes. Our host provided us with chairs, a table, and a fierce concoction of gin and beer, mixed in equal quantities.

1

Introduction

THIS BOOK is an account of my field study of a people of northern Uganda, the Lugbara, from the last days of 1949 to the fall of 1953, with two breaks in England during that period. It is not an autobiographical journal of my life among them; although nostalgically fascinating to myself, my diary would make dull and repetitive reading for anyone else. Nor is it a field-worker's *vade mecum*, a book on field techniques, except that it might be considered a book about a research study where the techniques used were both simple and traditional. It is a book about some aspects of methodology, those that I myself think are the important ones, and of the ways in which I collected certain kinds of information that I, as a social anthropologist, considered significant for understanding Lugbara society.

There are four statements to be made immediately, which I shall elaborate in the following chapters. The first is that I am a social anthropologist and am therefore interested primarily in understanding social relations—I am not a psychological anthropologist, nor an evolutionist anthropologist, nor any other variety. The second is that I have tried to give an account of what I did and by implication what I hoped and tried to do: this does not mean that what I did would necessarily be right for anyone else. Thirdly, if I were to make a study of the Lugbara now I would not do as I did sixteen years ago, nor would I hope and try to do what I hoped and tried to do then. Lastly, what I did was decided very largely by the Lugbara themselves: another people might have led me to do a different kind of research.

Anthropological research is extremely difficult and unlike any other kind of scientific work. We have a rigorous discipline in which amateur impressions and skills are not sufficient. We have to deal with people, not with objects in a laboratory, and people are a great deal more complex and difficult to understand than are molecules or nonhuman animals. We have to deal with living people

1

among whom we live and work; we do not rely for our data on objective records of human activity such as written documents, questionnaires or tapes of speeches, but upon actual observation of and participation in the activities of people who have no particular reason to be pleased that we are there and who have the power to ignore us, to snub us, or simply to get rid of us if they wish to do so. Throughout this book I stress the paradox of the anthropologist's having to live as a human being with other human beings yet also having to act as an objective observer. This is not an easy task and I certainly do not claim that I succeeded in it. I can only set down how I tried to resolve this paradox and the other problems, some personal, others those of collection and interpretation of anthropological experience, that faced me in the field.

The Choice of the Lugbara

As I have said, this is not a day-to-day diary of field research. I therefore divide this book into sections, in each of which one or two main points are made. In this chapter I wish to say something of why I chose the Lugbara for study and what I expected to get out of my stay among them.

At the end of the Second World War in Britain there was a great increase in the importance given to social anthropology and almost for the first time it became relatively easy to obtain money for fieldwork. I wished to do research and was lucky enough to be given funds by the Worshipful Goldsmiths' Company of London, a livery company or guild which made many grants for various educational projects. While they could not give me enough money to finance this kind of work completely, they gave me over half of what I needed. The remainder came from a grant from the Colonial Social Science Research Council, part of the research arm of the British Colonial Office. Today it is of course fashionable to suspect such moneys as committing the fieldworker to act as some kind of spy, but such naive suspicion would be unfounded in the case of the kind of work for which I was given the grant. I was never asked to do any specific research for anyone or any institution, except that the government of Uganda told me that they were interested in problems of labor migration and any information I could give them on that topic would be welcome. However, I was left completely alone to do my own work, to carry out my own projects and to do the research as I thought best.

I chose the Lugbara mainly for the simple reason that no anthropologist had ever worked among them, and I was romantic enough to want to find a relatively "untouched" society. There were two or three published articles by former missionaries and administrators, none being of any great value. The Lugbara live in a remote part of northern Uganda, a country that I had visited during the war and which held a great fascination for me. The fact that their language is related not to the other languages of East Africa but to those of what were then the Sudan and French Equatorial Africa was certainly a factor in my choice. In addition I knew that the Lugbara actually existed because I had met Lugbara troops during the war in various parts of East Africa and the islands. But other than their being tall, very dark-skinned, and apparently both cheerful and somewhat easily quarrelsome people, I knew little about them. By reading what was available I could learn a certain amount. I knew that their economy seemed technologically to be simple, that they lacked a king or traditional chiefs, that they appeared to have a somewhat complex religion in which various spirits, ancestors, and forms of divination featured prominently, and that in the years after 1912 they had had a prophetic movement that culminated in a small revolt in 1919, which was soon put down by the government of the time. I knew also that they were divided between the territories of Uganda and of the then Belgian Congo, and that they had formerly been part of the Lado Enclave during the later days of Arab slaving in the southern Sudan. They seemed suitably remote and unknown, and my teacher, Professor E. E. Evans-Pritchard, agreed that they would make an admirable first study where I could learn my job. I therefore applied to make a straightforward ethnographic study of this people.

It is more difficult to say what I expected to find. At that time my main interest was in political organization, and I realized that the Lugbara would provide an example of a politically uncentralized society of the type exemplified in my teaching by the Nuer and the Tallensi. At the time that seemed sufficient reason to visit them. Nowadays, of course, any such naive project would be frowned upon by departments of anthropology and most funding agencies. I think, looking back, that my teachers and I were correct in planning a virtually purely exploratory study of this kind. It is all very well to dream up a set of hypotheses and call them a project, which may persuade a foundation that the writer knows what he is talking about. But in practice the over-rigid definition of a project limits the value of the later work rather than enhancing it.

When I look back now on the beginning of my research I am astounded at much of my lack of preparation for what I was about to do. I do not mean by this that I was not trained properly, for in fact I had been lucky enough to have been given the best anthropological training that I could have found anywhere. It had been rigorous, sophisticated, and thorough, and I had been taught by six leading anthropologists all of whom were at the height of their powers. They all believed that the best way to train a young anthropologist was to teach him the subject and not to worry about techniques as such. In other words, I was given a thorough grounding in the subject but escaped being fed with the latest fads that so often beset the unfortunate students of today. However, and it may be that I am merely being wise after the event, I wish now that I had received a better training in linguistics and in what for lack of a better term I will call the philosophical background of anthropological observation. For example, I read, very belatedly, Collingwood's *The Idea of History* at the very end of my fieldwork while trying to make sense of Lugbara ritual. I wish that I had read it two years earlier. It was only after my field research was over that I realized the wisdom of my teacher, Professor Evans-Pritchard, when he maintained that social anthropology is a discipline that is best taken after a first degree in a subject such as history or philosophy.

The Journey to the Field

I need not say much about my getting to the Lugbara. I sailed from London to Mombasa, then took the train for the two days' journey to Kampala, in Uganda. There the principal of Makerere College generously offered me the hospitality of his house for a few days. His kindness enabled me to settle in Kampala for a week to take stock of the general situation. Since I had already spent four years in East Africa during the war, I knew a certain amount of the general social background of the region, and I regard this knowledge as an essential beginning for any field-worker. He must at least learn such things as the coinage, the nature of the government of the country, even such things as the names of stores, the kinds of food available and so on. These all provide a background which in one way or another proves valuable, as it is difficult to do research in a vacuum of any kind. During my stay in Kampala I visited the central government offices at Entebbe, the seat of government several miles away. There I was shown files and census materials to do with West Nile District, the home of the Lugbara. I found no one who had actually ever been to West Nile, but one or two officers had worked in other parts of northern Uganda and told me that it was remote and backward.

After a week I went to West Nile by road and by Nile steamer across Lake Albert. The District Commissioner offered me a bed in his house for a couple of days after which I moved into the government resthouse at Arua, the local district headquarters. I stayed there for five days before going out into the country-side. During that time I met the other officials, both English and African, the missionaries (both Catholic and Protestant) and the local storekeepers (mostly Indian), and was driven up and down the few roads of the district. It is fashionable today to think little of these colonial officials and to regard an anthropologist who would even talk to them, let alone accept their hospitality, as being disloyal to his scientific aims. This seems to me to be nonsense: one does not lose one's professional or personal integrity by being polite. Also one cannot study people in a colonial situation without taking into account the government, the missions, and the other influences that affect them in so many ways. I am not saying that I had to accept every view that was held at the time by local officials; I did not do so, and was usually regarded by them as at the least eccentric if not radical and even revolutionary. But they knew a good deal about the area, and I would have been merely self-righteous not to have accepted their help. The District Commissioner was responsible for me, in the sense that had I been sick or injured he would have to take care of me and make reports on me. I realized later that he was uneasy as to the effect my presence in his district might have; after having seen the behavior of one or two other visitors in Uganda and elsewhere, I now quite understand his uneasiness. He and the other officers of the administration proved themselves to be very helpful; they always treated me with the utmost propriety and kindliness, and never tried to prevent me from doing any research that I wanted to. During my stay in Arua I also visited Aru, the equivalent headquarters of the Lugbara areas in the Congo some fifteen miles to the west (Aru and Arua are Lugbara words meaning "jail"), and there made the acquaintance of the Belgian *chef de poste*, who was likewise to prove helpful in my later work.

After driving around the district for a few days I decided that I had to take the plunge as quickly as I could and start my actual work, even though I had spent merely one morning paging through some of the government files that were made available to me and knew virtually nothing of the language. I decided to move to an area fairly near to Arua, because there was an unused and somewhat tumbledown government camp there which I could use immediately until I could arrange to move out into the countryside. It seemed better to live there at the beginning rather than to spend any further time in Arua. I therefore set about acquiring some basic equipment such as a bed, a table, a chair, and a few utensils. I could have bought these in London before sailing for Uganda, but luckily had realized the absurdity of equipping myself as though a member of a Victorian expedition to the Dark Continent and had left it all until I reached the field itself. Most of my furniture was made for me in a couple of days by the local Catholic technical school, and it was far better than I could have bought in England, as well as being a tenth of the price. I acquired a map of the district, and some reams of paper from an Indian store in Arua. I hired a cook and a general factotum with the help of the Protestant mission. I also rented an ancient truck from the mission. A week or two later a rear wheel fell off while rounding a corner, and I then bought a more modern vehicle from the central government; this was made available to me since I was attached to the government for tax purposes. I therefore had a truck for my fieldwork, although in fact it was never used very much and spent much of its time as a model for a mechanics' class in the Catholic technical school, where it was kept clean and polished, both within and without, as though a precious museum piece.

One afternoon I mounted my vehicle with my cook and other assistant in the front and my small pile of living equipment in the back, and drove out to the place where I was first to begin work. I was made welcome by Sultan Obitre, the local government chief, somewhat confused as to my identity and role. Later when he discovered I was not a government official but merely wished to live somewhere in his chiefdom in order to learn about the history and habits of his people he became a very good friend to me; I owe much to him.

2

Being a Stranger

IN THIS CHAPTER I wish to give some account of the first few weeks, in which I began to learn the elements of the language and culture of the Lugbara. My account may make my experience sound more coherent than it actually was: at the time it seemed to be merely continual confusion. In fact, as I will show later, three quarters of my field material were gathered during the final months of my stay. The first year was really spent in trying to know enough of Lugbara culture to be able to see its main principles and emphases, and to learn what questions could be asked in order to make some sense and pattern out of the bewildering and often apparently chaotic life that I saw in front of me.

Here I wish to make four points with regard to a study of a people such as the Lugbara, assuming that the observer has the proper training, has some reasonably coherent aims in his study, and lives with the people whom he is studying with friendliness and courtesy. The first is that the fieldworker is like a young child and learns about the culture of the people in very much the same way as does a growing child in that culture. The second is that it is of no use trying to guide one's field research in particular directions. The people themselves open the doors to their culture, and since one does not know what these doors are or where they lead once opened, one can only wait and hope that this will be done. One cannot force the process, and at times the very haphazard nature of it makes one despair and think that one is getting nowhere. Sooner or later a pattern does emerge, but I am convinced that if one tries to force that pattern in certain directions then one is guilty of distortion and comes away with an inaccurate view of the total culture (although perhaps having solved a particular research hypothesis to one's own satisfaction). The third point is that despite the claims of many anthropologists, travelers, and other visiting observers, one is never absorbed completely into a strange society. It would be more accurate to say that if one is absorbed, he ceases to be an observer. The tightrope between cultural absorption and objective observation is a slender one and difficult to traverse. The last point is that the observer from another society can hope only to learn a very small amount

6

of the strange culture that he is observing, and so he has often to select what seems to him at that particular moment to be the most promising path and to ignore others. Most of the missionaries among the Lugbara obviously know far more about certain aspects of Lugbara life than I do: a man who has been there for forty years learns much that an observer who stays merely for two will never know. The strength of the anthropologist, however, is that by his training and by the fact that during his stay he has absolutely nothing else to do but watch what is going on around him, he is able to see relations between pieces of behavior and between various social institutions that may not be so obvious to other kinds of observers; his choice of the paths of inquiry to follow is never so haphazard as it might at first sight appear to be.

The Countryside

Before I describe my first few weeks it is useful to give a brief description of the countryside in which I lived. The landscape in Lugbara was always a central part of my everyday experience, as it is for the Lugbara themselves. It is a landscape very different from that of most other peoples of this region, and the Lugbara know this and point it out as being an important part of their cultural background. Lugbaraland is part of the high watershed between the Nile to the east and the tributaries of the Congo to the west. It is between four and five thousand feet above sea level, and one is soon conscious of living on a high and fertile plateau surrounded on three sides by river valleys and low dry plains—only to the south, in Alur country, are there hills higher than in Lugbaraland.

This plateau is both high and open. There are few trees; once the area was probably covered with thick woodlands but they have been cut out by the densely settled Lugbara farmers. Also there are few wild animals, in contrast to the surrounding areas that are thickly wooded and filled with leopard, buffalo, elephant, and rhinoceros. In the center of Lugbaraland rise the two massifs called Liru and Eti. These mountains feature in Lugbara myths and provide an ever-visible focus for the sense of being "we Lugbara." The remainder of the country consists of rolling plains and small ridges each separated by the many permanent rivers that cross the countryside and run either east into the Nile or west into the tributaries of the Congo. The watershed between the two rivers is the international border between Uganda and the Congo, and it is clearly marked on the ground by streams flowing from it in opposite directions. I soon had the sense of belonging to a single people; in clear weather they can see one anothers' clan homelands and even see one anothers' compounds many miles away across the landscape; in the planting season one can see in the distance the fires that are burnt to clear the bush. When I occasionally visited other parts of Uganda, accompanied by Lugbara friends, they would always note the differences of the countryside, saying for example that in Acholi across the Nile one could not see other compounds but merely winding paths vanishing into the bush; in the south and in the far west of the Congo they wondered at the thick forests where no one can see anything of his neighbors.

The Neighborhood

From where I was living I could see out across the undulating countryside. My hut was on a small rise from which I could see below me the compounds, each surrounded by its fence of plants and by its home fields, and between them the paths wandering to neighboring compounds. As far as my eye could see there were compounds and fields, on and on to the horizon. This is a thickly occupied country, very different from the surrounding regions, like a small island set on its high plateau and distinct in both its appearance and in the culture of its inhabitants. From the beginning I was aware of the need to understand the pattern of organization of these myriad homesteads set out as on a map before me. Just as Lugbara talk continually about the relations of clans and of villages, and of the historical migrations of their ancestors across their high plateau, so was I soon drawn into discussions of these important matters. One could not possibly ignore them and I was soon to realize that to make some sense out of this landscape was clearly my first important piece of work.

I started this merely by walking, some ten miles or so each day, with a companion, so as to see the kind of life that went on in the homesteads and fields that I could see from my ridge. Each day I would set out in a different direction, and this served the purpose of introducing me to large numbers of people who were naturally somewhat curious and suspicious of my being there at all. The Lugbara had never seen a European who walked so much, except for a few missionaries who visited the sick or dying, or occasionally an eccentric government officer, who was of course accompanied by a small party of chiefs and tribal police. I walked about with only one person, who was my general assistant and introducer. My conversations with the local people whom I met were naturally limited, because I could not easily understand what was said to me. I could converse using some Swahili, a language I had known for some years; and as I became more proficient I substituted Lugbara for that useful *lingua franca*. Most of the time I was treated with friendly amusement, except only by the children who after getting over their initial fear of me tried earnestly to teach me their language much as they themselves would teach it to their younger siblings. This provided me with an excuse to write words in a notebook, so that later the fact that wherever I went I would write down everything that I witnessed was accepted as a normal part of my behavior. I would also visit the local market, held near my hut twice a week; people soon grew used to my being there and accepted me as one of the local sights that could serve as a useful conversation piece.

People were not always friendly and amused. On my third day, hearing the sound of drumming a few hundred yards away, I walked down a path to find a death dance being performed. Several hundred people had collected from the surrounding countryside and were consuming immense quantities of beer and food. I was subjected to a great deal of fist clenching and spear shaking by the men, who thought that my intrusion into a mourning rite was uncalled for, and to spitting and cursing by the women, who feared that I would harm their babies by casting the evil eye on them. All one can do in such circumstances is to stand

Afetiya, Oguda's second wife, lining a new carrying basket with mud and dung. The framework for her new hut is in the background.

Co-wives of two generations. The woman in the foreground is making a serving tray of peeled sorghum stalks. Her co-wife (the mother of the little girl) sits immediately behind her, covering her face to hide her laughter—she is holding a woman's knife. The older women are the co-wives of their husband's father; the one in the background has a carrying-ring on her head and a lip-pin in her upper lip.

smiling somewhat oafishly and hope for the best, certainly giving up any idea of filling one's new notebooks with an elaborate analysis of the death dance itself.

By the end of ten days or so I had walked for five or six miles in each direction along the small paths that stretched out across the country. I was naturally an object of some fear, suspicion, and curiosity, but at least I was known to the people of the neighborhood and had some idea of their way of life and of the problems I should have to face in deciphering the pattern behind their everyday behavior. I knew certain things, which may now seem very simple and obvious but which were none the less essential pieces of knowledge that I did not have before and that served as a basis for my early attempts to understand Lugbara culture and social organization.

I knew that Lugbara huts were round and covered with thatch that sat above the mud and dung walls. A hut was the home of one wife and her children. A man might have more than one wife (I was later to learn that about a third of the men were polygynous) and usually the huts of his wives would be set within the same large compound; however, this was not always so and the huts of co-wives were often in separate small compounds separated by fifty to a hundred yards of field. The men told me that it is the nature of women to quarrel and therefore it is useful to separate them so that they cannot make one's life a misery. I knew that within the hut there was a mud and dung floor that was swept two or three times a day with small brooms of stiff grass. Usually there was a cooking fire in the hut, so that it was filled with smoke that found its way out through the blackened thatch. There would be a rough bed made of twigs covered by a papyrus mat, and the personal belongings of the occupants would be placed on the top of the wall or stuck in the inside of the thatch so that mice and other vermin could not reach them easily.

Outside the hut within the compound there were granaries of many shapes and sizes, each intended for a different kind of grain. The traditional staple was eleusine, a type of millet rich in protein and capable of being stored for many years. Other basic crops were various kinds of sorghum, sesame, beans, ground nuts, some maize, and a good many other crops of which I did not know the English names and which I always found difficult to recognize. My ignorance of what were to Lugbara their everyday plants was always to be a source of amazement and amusement to them; they could not believe that anyone could be so ignorant of such important matters. Under the granaries there were shrines, again of many shapes and sizes, the most common being small square houses, perhaps a foot in height, made of pieces of granite. Some of these had plants growing in them; some had small roofs made of thatch. They did not seem to be regarded as anything sacred, and often hens would scratch and children play and sit among them. I realized, however, that they were of great importance, and perhaps it was their very neatness of construction that attracted me to them, as one is attracted to a miniature model in our own culture. However, I clearly had to leave any study of shrines and religious beliefs until later when I hoped to know the language a great deal better. The huts and granaries were set on dried mud and dung floors which, like the floors of the huts, were kept clean and swept. Often a fire was made on the compound floor, around which I saw people sit to eat; in the evenings they would gather there to chat and to sing and listen to stories told by the older people. Usually the compound was surrounded by a high hedge, sometimes of sticks set in a circle but more typically of twigs that had taken root and were covered with leaves. There would be a space left for the entrance and from it paths led to neighboring compounds, perhaps two hundred yards away. Each was a small home of its own, clearly marked out from its neighbors and the center of everyday work and activities of the small family that occupied it.

Each Lugbara family had one or two goats, a sheep or two, perhaps one or two cattle, and always a dog, a cat, and some chickens. The larger animals were kept inside the compounds at night, tethered to stakes set in the ground, and during the daytime would be led off to pasture by the small boys of the family. I soon grew used to something of the daily round of everyday life. In the early morning, when it was still cold and when there was often frost, the world would wake and I would hear the calls of people as they prepared to eat the leavings of the evening meal of the day before, and the cries of the children as they drove the goats and cattle out into the fallow fields which were used as pasture. By eight or nine o'clock people were moving from their huts, men going to find beer-drinks and the women visiting each other or walking to the nearest marketplace (markets were held on most days, in a different place each day). People ate in mid-afternoon, and by dusk they would be in their homesteads. My favorite time of the day was from five to seven in the evening, when people had eaten and were willing and happy to talk, and when in the still weather the smoke of fires from the compounds would rise straight into the air. I could hear the sounds of the bells around the necks of the cattle and goats as they were driven home for the night, and would hear everywhere the faint hum of voices and calls as people settled down for the evening. Occasionally there would be the sound of singing and playing of harps and the shrill argument of co-wives and mothers trying to get their children to sleep. The Lugbara always said that no one moved from their homesteads after dark for fear of the witches that frequented the countryside at night; but in fact I soon discovered that most of the younger men were walking from their homes to those of the girls whom they would visit at nighttime. There would sometimes be the sound of drumming and singing from across the countryside when there was a moon, but by midnight all would be cold and still.

I began work at the very end of December, when there were no crops growing and when the people were waiting for the main rains to begin in March before they started to plant crops for the new season. This meant that at this time of the year the fields were mainly empty; later, in June and July, when the crops ripened, the compounds were to be surrounded by fields of sorghum, some varieties of which are eight or nine feet high and effectively hide the compounds from outside view. But in the dry season from December until the end of February the countryside was bare of crops and I could see merely compounds surrounded by dry dusty fields; also there was much heat-haze and often I could see no more than a couple of miles—later, when the rains had come, I could see a hundred miles and more. A few large fig trees dotted the landscape and on the tops of the many small hills were clusters of eucalyptus, cassia, and other recently introduced trees used for building and for fuel. One of the first things I tried to understand was the agricultural calendar; but I soon found that I had to wait for a full year to go by until I knew enough about crops and their uses, before I could achieve anything very meaningful.

There were also the signs of external contact. About half a mile from where I then lived was the house of the subcounty chief in whose area I was living—that of the county chief, who had been the first to welcome me on my arrival, being a couple of miles farther. His house was unlike the huts of ordinary people, being a square brick-built house with a red tiled roof. All chiefs had these houses built for them by the government, to give them prestige and to mark their high status. In most cases the chiefs used them as offices and storerooms, preferring to live in more traditional round mud huts set nearby. Near the chief's house was another, used as courtroom on Monday mornings and as a jail for the rest of the week and known locally as the "lock-up," one of the few English words known by all Lugbara. In it were always one or two prisoners, often allowed to return home to see their wives at nightfall and coming back punctually at six o'clock the following morning, and also the chief's goats, living in close amity with the prisoners.

Near the jail was a square compound of granaries filled with millet against the threat of famine. This was one of the more important tasks of the government chiefs, since before colonial rule famine came regularly every ten years to Lugbara-land. On the other side of the chief's headquarters was a small marketplace that was open twice a week where women came from many miles around to barter, to buy and to sell, to flirt and pass the time of day and spread the news of the country-side. This was one of the few places where the outside world impinged obviously upon Lugbara life, since the market was visited not only by local people but also by itinerant traders from Arua and women from the Congo; I soon realized that Lugbaraland was not entirely isolated from a wider region.

On my other side, beyond a eucalyptus copse, was a local evangelist's school. The teacher, who was to become a close friend, was literate and managed to teach the rudiments of western education to a few dozen somewhat unwilling small children. On Sundays the school was used as a church which was visited by the people of the neighborhood (most of whom were pagans) dressed in bright pieces of cloth and the younger girls wearing flowers in their hair. The church, like the marketplace and the dancing ground, was one of the few places where boys and girls could arrange dates for the coming week.

The Role of Stranger

At the end of two or three weeks I thus had acquired a very slight knowledge of the surface of everyday life. I had convinced myself that I was at least trying to do anthropological work and was not merely a tourist enjoying a few exotic scenes, but I was clearly a stranger. I wish to stress this, since to realize that one is a stranger is perhaps the first stage in recognizing one's objective status as an observer. As I was later to learn, the Lugbara say that a stranger (*atibo*) is not a person (*'ba*), but, like a newborn baby, only a thing (*afa*): once he recognizes that fact, he can begin to develop into a person by recognizing his obligations and by his hosts' and elders' recognizing his rights. I still had to use Swahili, so that any conversation was stilted and without much content. But I was at least learning something of the structure of the local neighborhood, and within it was able to place a few individuals whom I could by now recognize and treat as individuals rather than as members of an undifferentiated mass of strangers— after all, the relationship of the individual member of a society to the remainder of his society is perhaps one way of defining the basic field of analysis of the social anthropologist. I learned that the Lugbara, as far as my limited experience of them went, clearly recognized no differences of rank, were egalitarian and proud in their everyday relations with one another and yet recognized certain kinds of formal authority (which as yet I did not understand), and were careful and industrious farmers who were not averse to some hard drinking; except for the last, the women shared the same general qualities. Later of course, I was to modify this crude impression, but it is worth mentioning because I do not think that one can get very far in this kind of work without being affected by such impressions of everyday cultural behavior. This may not sound important, but what would one not give for even such a rough impression of the everyday behavior of the Greeks and Romans whose literature we have studied for so many generations? These early weeks were not wasted—although of course they were exciting at every moment—even though I wrote virtually nothing on my virgin sheets of paper.

The reactions of the local people to my presence were those of curiosity, suspicion, and fear. On the whole, everyone was curious about me. Very few people other than the chief, the schoolteacher, and some of the younger men who had been in the army during the Second World War, had ever spoken to a European. Thus my willingness to talk as an ordinary person rather than as one representing a distant and alien power was a source of amazement and puzzlement. This may sound rather patronizing, but it is merely a statement of fact. I was visited daily by many inquisitive people who wished to hear my stumbling attempts to greet them and to scrounge tobacco and anything else that I might possess or part with. I should add that people would also visit my hut and enter it when I was away walking elsewhere: on my return I would always find my smaller possessions moved, but even though I was sometimes away for a week or more, nothing was ever stolen or even broken—Lugbara enter other peoples' huts freely but to take anything would be an heinous offence. Many of the children were at first frightened to death of me and it was obviously a game of daring to see which children would venture near me, try a few words on me, and then run back to their giggling friends clustered at a safe distance from the ogre who had come to live among them. The older men were very puzzled by me; to them the European was a person of high status and power, and therefore Europeans were counted as old and senior men. I, however, was not old and clearly not senior for the simple reason that I did not give orders, and had furthermore asked Chief Obitre to tell people that I did not wish to have the semi-forced "gifts" of chickens, eggs, and firewood which were in those days normally given to visiting officials. The fact that I paid for everything brought to me set me apart from others. At first therefore the older men could not place me and had nothing to do with me. Later they were to find that I was a willing listener to their stories of the glorious past of their people and the situation changed radically. On the other hand, the old women had in most cases never spoken to a European nor shaken hands with one, and many of them had never set eyes on one. In fact my willingness to shake hands with everybody, rather like a visiting politician in this country—although a politician is not offered quite so many leprous hands as I was—showed that I was a decent-hearted person without airs of superiority. They therefore came to see me in droves, especially on market days when I soon realized I was an added attraction to any bargains to be made there, and exclaimed in wonder that the palms of my hands were so soft that it was clear that I had never done a decent day's work in my life. Many would stroke my arms and remark how surprising it was to feel so pleasant a human skin despite its unpleasant color. The younger women were also curious and wanted to see what sort of person I was by inviting me to go to dances with them, often turning up in small groups dressed in their best with flowers in their hair.

Many of the younger men thought that since I was neither government officer nor missionary I must have come there to acquire a farm for myself. They lived near the Congo border and knew of the acquisition of land in the Congo by Belgian settlers. However, once I had shown that I was not interested in land nor in trying to recruit them to work on the railways or on other labor projects in southern Uganda, the suspicion waned and they began to accept me as a person of their own age with whom they could talk and exchange beer and cigarettes without fear of offending me or of bringing down the anger of the government for making friends with me. Again, this may sound patronizing—but it is a fact of African history. On the whole the younger women were like the children. They were not suspicious of my motives, since to be suspicious was the duty of the men who protected them. But they were fearful that I had come to eat their babies. There were at the time three words in Lugbara for European or White Man. One, the usual one, was *Mundu*, the Lingala word for rifle: it was used for a European and also for people such as government chiefs, who although being Lugbara had the backing and power of the government. Another term, and an old-fashioned one, was *Ogard'ba*, literally axe-man: it referred to the fact that Europeans with rifles could cut people down as a man cuts down grass with a machete. The third term, also an old word and the one used by older men and women, was *Adro*, a word used for the immanent aspect of the Divine Spirit, that is believed to dwell in the bushland, to be tall and white-skinned, and to take people to eat them if they stray into his domain at nighttime. Europeans were considered to eat people, because they had the power of taking them to jail or of treating them in hospital, and as all Lugbara knew, some people who went to jail or to hospital never returned. Therefore, as I have said, the women would spit at me and snatch their babies from me. After a while, however, it became apparent that I was either very cunning and waiting my chance or that I was an exceptional European who did not eat babies. After a few weeks this fear evaporated in the same way that the suspicion of the men had done. It was obvious that to the end of my stay the Lugbara never accepted me fully as one of themselves. There is no reason why they should have done so, since although I was not an official nor a missionary, I was clearly an odd person. I was accepted as something *sui generis*, as a unique "non-European" who had come there simply because he liked to do so. After a year in the field I returned to England for five months, and my return to Lugbaraland was counted as proof of my affection for the people and as sign of my good intentions toward them. I was known to everyone as Dzonni, the nearest the Lugbara tongue can get to my given name, and was known generally as "our European," in distinction to other Europeans who occasionally impinged upon their lives.

3

Becoming a Kinsman

HAVING ACQUIRED some kind of friendly relationship with a few people, my next task was to understand something of the basic organization of the people among whom I was living. People like Lugbara have to absorb a stranger into a network of social relations or they cannot deal with him at all. The basic principle of interpersonal organization in their society is that of kinship; and relations within and between local settlements are seen in terms of kinship and clanship. I realized that if I were to be able to understand the pattern of their lives, as it exists for them, I would have to be absorbed to some extent into their system of kinship. At the time I did not do this deliberately, for the simple reason that I did not understand the system, nor am I implying that to be taken into a kinship system is necessarily the only or best way of learning a society's culture. But it is an effective means in the case of a people like the Lugbara. For them kinship is an all-pervasive idiom of social relationship, and a person is regarded and treated in certain ways either because he is a kinsman of a certain kind or because he is not a kinsman. There are no other basic categories of such significance for them.

Acquiring Kin

After I had been there for a few days I realized that besides learning the language the other immediate essential was to acquire someone who would always be with me and who would act as my sponsor and introducer. The first man that I used for this purpose had been recommended to me by Sultan Obitre and chosen by him for the simple reason that he had been a soldier in the army and a labor migrant for many years in southern Uganda. It was thought that he therefore "knew the words of Europeans." He was in fact a carpenter and thus an atypical Lugbara in that he was a trade specialist. He was a pleasant person, although something of a drunkard; but I did not like him. In any event he soon left to work

16

elsewhere in the district for the Public Works Department. I therefore looked around for someone else. Clearly he would have to be a fairly young man, since senior men would not work for me in any case; he had also to be someone who was well enough respected by his seniors for them to accept his sponsorship of me and my work, someone who knew a reasonable amount about his own culture and who would be introspective and objective enough to be able to understand what I wanted to know, and someone honest and likable enough for me to be able to trust and to enjoy being with for a considerable time.

After a few days I met a friend of my cook, or to be more accurate a distant "brother" of the girl whom my cook had met on our second day there and who was later to become his fifth wife. This girl Drabezu ("death carries away") had met Enosi, my cook, when walking down the path to the market with her clansman Oguda ("the stolen one"—because, as his mother later told me, at his birth his father had accused her of adultery because his feet were of a different shape than his father's). Oguda had, as did many Lugbara men, an "English" name, Wilson. I do not know where he got this name and he was no longer sure himself, but he was known by it to a large range of friends and neighbors, and took pride in it since it showed him to be a man who had been south as a labor migrant and who therefore knew the ways of the wider world. I asked Oguda if he would care to meet with me every day and to work for me for a full wage, to walk with me and in general look after me. He agreed to do so. He was with me for the remainder of my stay in Lugbaraland and became one of the closest friends I have ever had.

Oguda knew everyone in the area; he soon realized something of the nature of my work and could explain it to other people. Because I employed him it was thought that I had authority over him; he was therefore as a son to a father, I being the father. His real father was therefore my brother, his mother was my sister-in-law, his children my grandchilden, and so on. Within a few weeks I thus had a large circle of quasi-kin. Everyone knew of course that they were not "true" kin, but since in Lugbara the idiom of close social relationship is that of kinship this was for them the easiest way to place me in the local system and so to deal with me. It was in the beginning something of a joke and indeed I at first took it to be so. But I soon learned that there was much more to it than this. This happened one evening when Oguda's father's brother, who was the senior member of that family, came to me and talked with me about the behavior of Oguda and Oguda's elder brother; this was a rather quiet and serious man who was disturbed by the fact that by working for me Oguda had apparently acquired higher prestige than himself. I was responsible for Oguda's behavior since I was *in loco parentis*. This term, which we use ourselves when referring to the authority of a teacher over a pupil, does not adequately translate the relationship that the Lugbara gave me with regard to Oguda. I *was* his father in the situation of walking around the countryside with him. And I soon found that wherever we went, people who could trace some kinship link with him could thereby do the same with me, and promptly did so. This was translated into action. For example, one morning an aged crone came to see me with a gift of shea butternut oil that she was taking to the men of Oguda's lineage as repayment of a debt incurred to them some years before by her sister who had recently died. The old lady knew clearly that to bring this to me was not necessary. But it was for her an interesting way to make my acquaintance, a way of showing Oguda's kin that she was doing all she possibly could to repay her debt, and a means of putting me under an obligation for the future; and it was also the proper thing for her to do.

From then on in the area in which we lived I generally became known also as Nyiomva, literally "the child of Nyio," the name of Oguda's lineage. I was expected to behave to other people as if I were a member of that lineage by the giving of proper gifts and so on, and I did my best to carry out my expected role. This was expressed in many ways. I have mentioned the giving and exchange of gifts, but I noticed that on many occasions when observing a death dance, or sitting in a beer house, or attending a sacrifice, that if I did not stand near the people of Nyio sooner or later someone would gently remind me that that was where I should be. I have no doubt that some of the more wily men of Nyio realized that they benefited considerably by this channel to what seemed to them my limitless wealth. But it did enable me to acquire a position of some kind in the local community and also to be given gossip of a fairly scandalous and confidential kind about the many people whom the men of Nyio regarded as their enemies. Of course my position had the disadvantage that other people were perhaps not so willing as they might have been to regale me with their pieces of scandalous and confidential information about the people of Nyio. Yet in fact they would usually do so since in that situation they realized that I was not a "true" member of Nyio. I also found out very soon that it was necessary sometimes to stand well outside the situation. For example, I was asked by a man of Nyio to intercede for his son with the local chief who was to try him in his court on a charge of assault, but I did not do so. I therefore to some extent cheated on the implicit agreement. I do not necessarily recommend that a fieldworker become identified with one particular group or another. I mention all this merely to show the ways in which the Lugbara accepted me and my presence among them, rather than as an ideal method of acquiring information as an observer.

It was at this time that I began to be accepted locally as not only a human being but also as a social being, one who could be talked with and treated as a person who although knew few of the customs and little of the behavior of his hosts, was at least trying to learn them. I was told many months later, by an old lady who was a diviner and who taught me the rudiments of her art, that at the beginning I was not really a mature person at all. I was not 'ba, a person, but afa, a thing. As I have said, a baby and a client, just as a poor stranger who comes to attach himself to a richer man in time of famine, are not persons but things. They are things because they are immature, because as not being full persons they are worth little and cannot act responsibly. They may have owners, as do all things, but are not full members of the society, and traditionally the killing of them merited no punishment or vengeance. In other contexts women may be "things," that is, in those jural situations in which responsibility for them is held by men. I also began as a thing and was socialized to become a person by learning the language and the customs of my hosts. A baby and a stranger have many characteristics in common, that are shared by very old and senile people who are often referred to by Lugbara as ancestors and sometimes as things. They cannot speak properly, they cannot respond to what is said to them, they cannot always feed themselves, they do not know or they forget how to behave properly on ceremonial and ritual occasions, and so forth. I was of course in this position. My knowledge of the Lugbara language was at that time minimal and consisted mainly of asking questions as to what was in Lugbara the term for such and such an object. I did not know how to behave properly when entering a house, when eating, when dancing, when drinking, and of course above all when attending sacrifices and death rites. I had to learn these things in a few months, things that take babies years to learn. The comparison may seem fanciful but it is not. Certainly I must admit that at the time I was not aware of the exact process by which I was becoming acceptable as a socially responsible and adult being. But looking back I can see clearly the stages in this process.

The Behavior of a Kinsman and Neighbor

There were certain activities in which I began to take part after I had been there a few weeks. At first I assumed that these were merely pleasant things to do, which helped people accept me as an ordinary person who need not be feared or disliked, and which helped me not feel too isolated in this strange culture. But when I look back I realize that there was a great deal more of significance than merely being liked. These were activities that represented for the Lugbara actions of a kinsman and neighbor, as distinct from those of a stranger or an enemy. The first was that of eating and drinking with my hosts. Obviously any traveler may be invited into somebody's house in the country that he is visiting and may be offered a meal there. If he is courteous he will accept the invitation whether or not he likes the food. And that is how I regarded the first few invitations I had to eat in Lugbara homesteads. But, as I say, the invitations represented more than mere friendship.

The first man who asked me in to eat with him and his family was Toba, a member of Nyio lineage. Toba was rather a buffoon and generally regarded as a drunkard. He was one of those people who for a time becomes an acquaintance and whom one sees for many hours of the day without achieving any intimacy. Later on he and I were to lose touch completely. Oguda and I were walking one evening when Toba met us and invited us to enter his compound. Naturally, I did so, as this was the first friendly invitation I had received to enter a Lugbara house. It was to take several months before I was able to walk unconcernedly into a Lugbara compound. There was always the feeling of intrusion, of stopping everyday life for a few moments because of my strangeness or because of the fact that the small children would scream and run to their mothers for protection against the evil-colored stranger entering the gateway. In fact it did not take very long before the local children accepted me completely; but for the first few weeks this was always a trial for me. First I would enter the gateway in the compound hedge, and greet the people sitting on the compound floor who would ask me to sit down with them. Occasionally everybody would be inside the hut: I would then stand outside and ask to be invited in, a request that was never refused. I would bend low to get through the small doorway and come into the hut, usually occupied by what seemed at first to be a crowd of staring and inquisitive though friendly people sitting in near-darkness. This was always an ordeal. Once I was inside I would be asked to sit, a girl would bring warm water in which I would wash my hands, and beer or sometimes tea would be brought for me to drink. I would talk for half an hour or so and leave with protestations of friendship and esteem on each side, or be invited to stay and share whatever food was being prepared at the time. A distinguished guest, as I was in households that did not know me very well, was invariably offered a meal which might take two or three hours to prepare. Finally, the food would be served, consisting of porridge of millet, sorghum, or maize, accompanied by various relishes made of chicken or goat and with a groundnut, bean, or sesame sauce. I always found Lugbara food agreeable, except for the stronger goat's flesh and for the intestines and other offal. It was a sign of respect and affection by my host for him to share a particular piece of meat with me, by himself eating a small piece of it and then pressing the rest into my mouth or into my right hand. I found the Lugbara were always kind and welcoming, despite my own obvious failures of simple good manners through my ignorance of their etiquette.

One evening, therefore, we were asked to eat in Toba's house. I entered with some trepidation, being unsure of how to behave, but soon felt at ease because Oguda whispered directions to me for sitting, eating, and conversing politely. Later he was to show me how to belch properly after a meal to show my appreciation of it; but that took me some time to be able to do with *sangfroid*. After our meal we left shaking hands with joy and friendship on our way out of the homestead and accompanied by Toba to the borders of his fields. We then returned home. The next morning my hut was swamped with callers, all asking me to visit them to eat with them that evening. After discussion with Oguda, Enosi, and other well-wishers it was apparent that by eating with Toba (after all, hardly a very momentous act) I had shown my hosts several things. I had shown that unlike other Europeans in their experience I was willing to eat with them. This may sound complacent and patronizing, but it is not intended to be that: I am merely reporting what was told me by the Lugbara of that period. Secondly, I had shown that I trusted my hosts not to poison me. I was not to realize the full import of that statement until rather later when I became fully aware of the fears of sorcery among my neighbors. And thirdly I had shown that I could behave as could a kinsman. To share food is the epitome of kinship and to eat of a man's salt shows that one accepts the relationship of kinship that cannot later be denied. After that time, in fact, I would eat a meal every day with one friend or another. Often I would invite people to eat or drink with me, but this was not really expected of me since it was known that I had no wife to cook for me and to act as my hostess. Instead I returned hospitality by giving beer to the men in the various beer houses that I would visit each day, and to the women by giving gifts of a few cents when I met them at markets.

At first I admit that I found it difficult to drink the beer in any quantity due to its strong smell and the amount of dirt and foreign matter in it; also I found it difficult to drink from a calabash that had just been cleaned by the woman who was offering it to me having licked its rim before filling it. But I soon realized that to refuse beer would be both an absurdity and an insult, and as far as I know I never came to any harm from doing so. I would be offered a calabash of beer by the woman kneeling in front of me, I would take a few mouthfuls and then hand it to whomever was most senior in the circle. He likewise would take a draught and hand it to the next senior man; to hand it back to the donor would be an insult. Beer-drinks were regular occurrences. This was mainly because a woman who prepared beer for a given occasion usually made too much and would then either have to throw it away or sell it for a few cents' profit. Beer-making was the staple cottage industry of the women, who took their heavy pots of beer to regular beerhouses where they sold it, giving a percentage of their take to the owner of the beerhouse. The consequence was that for many men life consisted of drifting from one beer-drink to another day after day and I have known men who ate virtually no solid food at all, relying for sustenance on this thick and nutritious beer. As with food, my willingness and indeed my apparent love of drinking beer (which I admit was a simulated affection) was taken as a sign that I was willing to accept my neighbors as equals, as unwilling to poison me, and as kin and friends. Undoubtedly the fact that I seemed to have an unlimited supply of cents with which to buy beer was also an important factor. My hand may have become unsteady in trying to write down the conversations that I heard in beerhouses, but a great deal of my information came from those occasions.

Besides beer the Lugbara made an illicit liquor called *waragi* or "Nubian gin" (because the most skillful makers were Nubi women who lived in Arua Town). It was made secretly in stills set up in the makers' huts. I knew that it was prepared in the area where I lived, because I had been told so by the District Inspector of Police. He, an ex-London police officer, warned me against it and told me in a friendly manner that if I drank it it would be my own undoing; he turned a deaf ear to reports that I did drink it. One evening I entered a hut where it was being made, and was offered a tumbler full as it came hot from the still. *Waragi* was drunk from European-style tumblers, as it was considered a "European" liquor. It was clear that this was a test of my role, to see whether or not I reported it to the police. I did not do so, because I felt it would be wrong and because the hasty consumption of two glasses made me as drunk as I have ever been in my life. I can still remember staggering home, stepping carefully over the lintel of my hut and falling asleep until the next morning. This was regarded with high favor by my neighbors who exclaimed that I had been hit by the gin as though by a buffalo. It may have given me a headache but it set me apart from other Europeans as a man to be trusted in such matters.

The next activity was dancing. The Lugbara have several kinds of dance. The most traditional and most formal is the *ongo*, that is danced at a man's death by his kin. It was an *ongo* that I had visited on my third day when I was shown that I was feared and unwelcome. There is the *nyambi*, danced only by women at mourning. There are also two forms of dance that the Lugbara say are "modern." One is the *koro*, danced only in northern Lugbaraland and denounced by the missionaries as being obscene. The other is the *walangaa*, danced in central and southern Lugbaraland where I was living. It is not danced at a death but only for pleasure, and is an occasion for general singing, flirtation, and drunkenness. It is usually danced at the end of a market day, often in the marketplace. Men and unmarried girls (and some married women) take part. The first few occasions I went to a *walangaa* I stood meekly at the edge of the dance watching the general din, noise, and dust. About three weeks after my arrival a *walangaa* was held in my honor in front of my hut. This again was something of a test, since it was known that missionaries disapproved of this dance which they maintained led to much seduction and adultery. It always seemed to me that seduction and adultery would have taken place with or without the *walangaa* to help them on, and I must say that I could see no possible evil in these dances. The dance given for me meant that I had to take part, and finally, helped on by one or two glasses of gin and much urging by my friends, I entered the dance. I forgot my own sense of dignity and did the best I could. Despite my clumsiness, this was greeted with much approval and enthusiasm. A few weeks later I bought three drums, the treble drum or daughter, the tenor drum or mother, and the bass drum or grandmother, which I kept in my hut and brought out on Saturday evenings after market for people to dance near my home.

One dances with one's kin, in my case the men of Nyio, a row of men dancing in front of a row of girls. One by one the men would move forward to dance individually with the girl opposite, and then fall back while the next man would step forward. Although it is dirty and sweaty, noisy and dusty, it was great fun and I always enjoyed it despite the foolish impression that I must have given while doing so. One response was that I was known far and wide as the European who danced, and often walking down a pathway I would meet people in a field who at the sight of me would throw down their hoes and start dancing as a sign of welcome. Later my kin and I would go as a group to neighboring areas to dance competitively with other groups, to sing topical songs and generally to show that I was an unassuming human being who was willing to behave as did other people. The fact that my reputation as a dancer spread so far and fast was significant of the importance Lugbara gave to this human but politically unimportant activity.

There was another activity that was distinct from that of taking notes that I consider was important. This was the treating of sick people from the neighborhood. People such as Lugbara were always sick, with malaria, dysentery, sores, yaws, wounds of many kinds, and the more serious diseases such as leprosy, meningitis, and sleeping sickness. Although I had no medical knowledge, I did have medicines. The local government doctor, a European who ran the large government hospital single-handedly and who spent all his spare time traveling around his district investigating such things as sleeping sickness and anthrax, supplied me with a few simple drugs. Although they were originally intended for my own use I could hardly keep them for myself. Every day people would come to me to ask for medicine. All I could do was give aspirin and to dress the more dreadful looking sores and cuts brought to me. I soon realized that the flood of patients was unending, so I set aside an hour each morning to give what help I could. This meant that from seven until eight each day I would help, as best I could, several dozen people.

The favorite medicines were iodine and acroflavine, a yellow liquid intended primarily for dressing burns but with strong antiseptic qualities. I merely daubed everything in sight with the stuff. Whether or not my work had any good effect I do not know, but it could not have done harm, and was at least another sign of my willingness to act as a human being. Also I cannot imagine anyone not wishing to help the many unhappy and wretched people who came to me. After three or four months I organized a small dispensary, which was held every Saturday morning at the time of the local market. The doctor I have mentioned sent out an African nurse to treat patients at a small hut which my neighbors built when I told them that I could arrange some medical help for them. Most of the cases who came to the dispensary were women who were pregnant or had small children who suffered from dysentery or malaria. I had both gratitude and immense respect for the nurses who came out to help me do this, and their work and kindness became famed over a wide area. This work may not have helped me directly with my field research (although it gave me the opportunity to discuss Lugbara notions of sickness and curing), but it was one small way by which I could return some of the hospitality shown to me.

Material and Symbolic Culture

During this early time I started one reasonably planned study, that of material culture and technology. It is, and was then, somewhat unfashionable to devote much time to this aspect of culture, at least in the case of British social anthropologists. But I had received some training in this field in England and my teacher had, after all, written one of the few sociologically oriented accounts of material culture in his book *The Nuer.* I realized well enough that I could hardly expect to understand very much about technology without a thorough understanding of the basic social organization, which I could not hope to have for many months. But to make a start was something, and would, I hoped, lead to a quicker entrée into the culture of the people since I would at least have some basic knowledge of their way of life if I knew something of its technology.

I began by learning the Lugbara words for any object that they used and that I saw on my daily walks and visits. I then learned of what it was made, for what it was used, who made it and under what conditions, who used it and under what conditions, whether it was sold and if so what was its price, and so on. From this work I learned several things: that the "price" was usually determined for occasional market sale and had little or no relation to the "prices" of other objects; that time and labor were not counted in determining the price; that the price varied according to the social relationship between seller and buyer, or maker and buyer. In addition, some objects could be widely sold, others not at all or very rarely, the distinction being that of the ritual or ceremonial value of the object and not the difficulty of making it or of obtaining its raw materials. Of course, the basic principles were as obvious to me then as they are now, but I mention this stage in my work as there is a more important conclusion to be drawn from it.

I could see reasonably clearly that I had to enter that door into their culture which the people themselves were willing to open for me. At first also I was not able to understand very much of that culture, both because I could not speak the language well enough and also because I did not understand its basic principles of organization. Therefore I could not easily understand the symbolic aspects of it, which were what I was really after in my research. But I could comprehend a good deal of the nonsymbolic aspects, that were exemplified by technology and material culture. I was doing what a child does when he first becomes aware of the material objects around him that he can learn to manipulate and understand; in time he comes also to realize that these have symbolic importance, in that they encapsulate social relationships. But before he reaches that stage he can still make some sense out of his experience merely by manipulating them: he learns to do so "correctly" as he learns the symbolic attributes associated with them.

I tried also to learn as much as I could about farming and crops, and ways of tending livestock. I soon saw that to achieve much in these fields, from the point of view of an anthropologist, necessitated a knowledge of the organization of family and descent groups that I did not yet possess. Virtually the simplest techniques of farming and livestock-keeping were closely linked to rules of inheritance and allocation of land and livestock, and to matters such as the sexual division of labor, which I found not as easy as I had assumed they would be. The main reason was simple: the division of labor between men and women was sanctioned and comprehended by Lugbara themselves in terms of a cosmology which at that time I was not capable of grasping. In some respects this was of course basically a semantic problem—what was the significance of "woman" in Lugbara ways of thought?

I started also to try to estimate and measure the areas of various kinds of fields, yields of crops, and so on. This was not easy. First, I realized immediately that the Lugbara were often shocked and frightened at the thought of my measuring their land; later, when I was to return in 1953 with a small team, there was no objection at all, but by that time I myself had become well enough known to be trusted not to try to enclose and alienate land. Besides the difficulty of measuring the size of the many small and irregularly shaped fields, there was the virtual impossibility of estimating exact yields of crops all of which were planted in mixed stands so as to reduce erosion. But I could at least make out agricultural calendars and learn something of Lugbara techniques and beliefs about crops and farming. I soon saw that here also a great deal of the significance of farming for the people was in the ritual associated with it, and I could see that without a knowledge not only of the more agronomic aspects of the subject but also of sorcery, cosmological space, and of the powers of Divine Spirit I could not get very far. Again, I had to decide to wait until these matters were shown to me, and temporarily closed the notebook I had so confidentially opened on "Agriculture."

It was clear that I should also try to estimate the volume of exchange of various commodities at markets, the composition of household budgets and use of food and other goods. I soon found that I could easily collect a great deal of information, which could be added up and correlated in almost any way I wanted. But when I later got to know more about the ever-changing composition of families, households, and settlements, and about the kinship and lineage systems associated with them, I realized that these figures were largely useless. I had merely

A market in A'dumi. The line of women offering various grains for sale are the wives of a single small lineage. The woman in the immediate foreground has her baby in a leather sling, and is holding the "sunshade" which is normally placed over the baby's head.

counted things, without realizing that "things" are also vehicles of communication which acquire much or most of their significance because of the social relations represented in their use and exchange. I was on more than one occasion later to witness various brief visits by economic and agronomic experts, who did the same kind of brief study and returned home to produce largely erroneous conclusions without being forced later to revise their first findings in the light of more intensive understanding of the social fabric of the people whose economy they had tried to separate out as something to be observed in isolation. I was more fortunate: I had more time to spend and I had been given a better training for the analysis of the social life of peoples other than my own.

My regular observation for several weeks of these mundane but basic matters was an essential early step in my longer study. I spent what was probably too great a proportion of my time at markets, both at those held near where I was living and at others within a five or six mile radius. I was here able to meet people from a wide neighborhood, who showed curiosity about me and from whom I gathered, in a rather haphazard way, a sense of overall everyday behavior. I could watch and listen to people greeting, buying and selling with kin, neighbors, friends, and strangers; see the minute variations of adornment and cicatrization that marked subclan areas; see the various crops and goods that were regarded as necessary or useful enough to merit barter or sale at markets. Since a Lugbara market, like most markets anywhere in Africa, is an occasion for general social intercourse as well as exchange of commodities, my presence was not regarded in itself as anything very strange; many people spent hours at markets without buying or selling anything. I was soon to find that many acquaintances would meet me regularly at the market nearest my home, and that it was generally expected that I would be there. In brief, for several months my usual presence at the market gave me some kind of easily comprehensible status as far as a wide neighborhood was concerned—comprising perhaps two or three thousand people.

Europeans and Others

This kind of life was often a lonely one. At times I longed to speak English and talk with people who were not Lugbara nor themselves immediately involved in Lugbara culture. Obviously some of these were other Europeans and I should say something about them since they were, or at least their presence was, an integral part of my research. There were three categories of these Europeans. First were the members of the Uganda Administration. At the time of my stay these were seven in number, all living in Arua Town, some dozen miles from where I was then living.

It was obvious to the Lugbara that I, unlike they, could go to Arua and talk with the various officials there. I was regarded as "our European," the man who could be used as a messenger to the source of power. I was consistently asked by chiefs, subchiefs, teachers, and many disgruntled persons to intervene on their behalf in one way or another with government officials. In fact I refused to do so except on two occasions. The dilemma of wishing to ask for administrative redress in cases of injustice and yet of not wishing to make use of one's position in this respect must at one time or other face every anthropologist. The anthropologist sees the consequences of administrative decisions, many of which lead to small local injustices which could seemingly be put right very easily by a word in the right quarter. Yet the anthropologist, of all people, cannot make use of his position. I am, as I have said, speaking here of my own work in a colonial situation; but the same applies to any fieldworker at one time or another. One occasion to which I refer was when I observed the semiannual sleeping sickness inspection of the entire population, at which medical orderlies toured the countryside to make a cursory inspection of every man, woman, and child. I discovered that the orderly concerned was charging money for the inspection, those who could or would not pay being beaten. I heard of this happening, and saw it with my own eyes and thought that this should be stopped. I reported it to the medical officer, and the orderly responsible was charged and removed from duty. The other occasion in which I was directly involved was when I was awakened in the middle of the night by a drunken and blood-stained man who told me that he had speared his brother thinking that his brother was a witch in the guise of a leopard. I persuaded the man to stay in my hut until the morning, when after discussion with him and others I took him to the local police officer at Arua and said that he wished to give himself up for the killing of his brother. He was given a probationary sentence only, whereas otherwise he might have been tried for murder. In general, I did not regard it as my duty to interfere with the judicial processes which were in the hands of the chiefs and the administration. I had my own ideas as to justice and injustice, the latter being frequent, but did not consider (and I think that I was right) in interfering unless the injustice became too great.

I would visit the district township every other week to collect my mail, to cash a check (there was no bank, so I used the government office, the Lugbara believing that I was able to get any sums I desired merely by asking for them, which made my frequent protestations of having no more cash to distribute sound rather hollow), and to buy a few supplies at one of the local stores. I think that I was remiss in not studying the members of the administration more objectively. There was little everyday contact between them and the people, but the indirect effects and influence of their work were of course considerable. I would often sit in a compound and see on the horizon the dust of an official's car passing down the road from Arua to Aru in the Congo. It emphasized the remoteness of the outside world, and had the same degree of reality as did the plane that flew far overhead every Friday morning at eleven o'clock from Stanleyville in the Congo to Juba in the Sudan. It was a sign that an outside world existed, but a world that impinged hardly at all in any direct or immediate sense on that of the Lugbara and myself.

The second category of European consisted of English Protestant and Italian Catholic missionaries. Almost all of them were based on the two mission stations in Arua, although a few lived in out-stations in various parts of the district. I myself had not approved of missionary aims, but I had soon to admit that the individual missionaries were kind and generous men who did what they thought was right with regard to the culture which was in many ways their duty to destroy. Again, it is fashionable to decry missionaries and certainly I would admit that in my experience many of them behaved foolishly, ignorantly, and harmfully with the people whom they regarded as their charges. I would add that the fact that they lived with little of the affluence associated with Europeans and that they were good and kindly people had a considerable effect. Neither they nor in this particular district the officers of the central administration were in their everyday behavior the overbearing agents of an all-destroying civilization. Lugbara realized from observing them, which they did very carefully, that Europeans could be human beings as they were themselves and could be both good and bad as individuals.

The third category of Europeans consisted of a few tobacco growers and buyers. Although their reputation was known widely they kept to themselves and had little effect on Lugbara except as employers of a few laborers.

There were also Indian and Arab storekeepers and traders. They kept small stores in Arua and at the time of the tobacco and cotton harvests would go out into the countryside as buyers. Although conventionally regarded in east Africa as exploiters, they played an important role in the history of the district, having been established there since the time of the First World War. They were channels for the introduction of consumer goods such as cigarettes, clothing, kerosene, soap and other small commodities, and also of cash, playing the role of bankers in an area with no banks. Their everyday influence on Lugbara culture was, however, minimal.

In my immediate neighborhood there were a few people who stood outside traditional Lugbara life. I have mentioned two of them, one being the local county chief and the other the local Protestant evangelist. Both were members of the category known to the Lugbara as the "New People," those who had contact with European knowledge and power and who thereby regarded themselves as cut off from the local people among whom they worked. They were sent by the administration or the missions to live in areas where they had no kin affiliation and were members of an incipient class of educated and western-oriented people set apart from the traditional culture of the Lugbara. I admit that it took me some time to become aware of the role of the New People as the agents of change, the intermediaries between Lugbara and the all-powerful outside world.

Not far from where I first lived there were two small African-owned stores, both selling cloth and soap and other domestic goods, and both with sewing machines. One was kept by a Kakwa, the other by a Lugbara from another area. They had both been in the army and had long histories of labor migration. They were the only entrepreneurs in the locality, and although they stood outside the traditional culture and also were excluded from the system of power controlled by the administration and the missions, they had considerable everyday impact on local life. They were at first very suspicious of me, partly because they thought I would spy on their gin-selling and other small irregularities and also because for a time I was to steal their thunder as representatives of an outside world associated with flashy consumer goods. It was not very long, however, before we were on good terms, and would spend a good deal of time talking about trade and army life while drinking European beer and *waragi* gin. The elderly Kakwa storekeeper had a disreputable wife, a stout and heavy-drinking lady known locally as "*mukora* number one," *mukora* being the LuGanda word for "whore." This referred not so much as to her personal behavior in its literal sense as to the facts that she wandered around from market to market and that her elder daughter was said to merit the term. She was a friendly soul and attached herself to me for a time as guide and mentor, but dropped me when she found I did not need her services as liquor supplier and procuress.

Finally there was the Goan customs officer who ran the lonely customs post on the Uganda-Congo border. He and I became friends and would go together to Aru in the Congo whenever I decided to stock up on food and drink there rather than in Arua—Aru could provide Portuguese wine and French cheeses. I would also visit him every other week or so to drink brandy and ouzo with him and discuss matters of mutual interest, mainly the respective glories of western Europe and Goa. I owe much to him and hope that I relieved his sense of isolation as much as he did mine.

At this period I did not take as much notice as I later realized that I should have done of these figures from outside the traditional Lugbara world. One reason was that I was then principally concerned to understand as much as I could of that traditional world—and remember that it had not changed all that much, certainly not as much as had the great majority of the societies of east Africa—and was not so interested in modern developments. I was to change that view before I left Lugbaraland. Another reason was that during these first nine months or so I regarded many of the figures of this outside world as people with whom I could drop the role of objective observer and return to that of an ordinary and unthinking person. The training of an anthropologist, rather like that of a psychiatrist, has as one of its main aims to enable one to be an observer of any situation at any time; at this period I had not completed my training which is achieved only by a full period of field research. I am not saying that since then I have been an efficient and objective observer of every scene I have experienced— I should not wish to become such a person even if I could do so. But at the time I am describing I was changing my role in this respect and was therefore in an uncertain and transitory state, and so often grateful to be able to revert to behavior that was for me usual and easy. As the time wore on I became less and less dependent on the outside world and more able to sink myself in Lugbara culture for long periods.

4

Understanding the Wider Society

A s I WROTE at the beginning of this book, it is not a diary. There is little value in merely listing the small pieces of information that I collected from day to day and that I was later to put together after I had left the field and begun to write up my material. But some aspects of Lugbara social life became apparent sooner than others. This was to some extent deliberate on my part, since as I have mentioned it became clear very early that without a grasp of the basic principles of Lugbara social organization I could understand comparatively little of their culture. Many anthropologists do not accept this view, and early in their field research begin to make elaborate analyses of such things as the individual personality of the people they are studying or of ideological and cosmological notions. However, I believe that one cannot understand these matters adequately without first understanding the basic social organization. Without that knowledge one tends to base one's analysis too much on one's own notions and assumptions as to values and ideologies rather than relying on those of the people themselves. Besides a knowledge of the basic social structure one must of course have an adequate knowledge of the language: I take this as a given. In my case I was not able to understand Lugbara with any degree of competence until I had been there for nine or ten months. Lugbara is a difficult language and I had to learn it as I went along.

The Structure of the Landscape

The open Lugbara landscape spread out in front of me made me realize that to understand it I had to find a pattern in it. At first sight the countryside was covered with myriad small hamlets stretched out as far as my eye could see; yet I noticed that the Lugbara had various ways of making a pattern out of this apparent confusion. They did this in several ways. The first that I learnt from them was made by using certain topographical notions. The area to the east they would refer to as "Low," and that to the west as "High." The area in the center of the country around the two mountains that rise from the plateau they would refer to as the "vagina" of their country. They said that it was from that area that came their ancestors who, with the many generations of their descendants, had spread out across the countryside to form the pattern that lay in front of us when we looked out over the landscape. This covered the entire region, stretching perhaps a hundred miles, that we could see.

There was also a pattern within each small local neighborhood. My first stage in understanding this was to learn something of the network of relationships that composed the basic residential unit. A man would be the master of one homestead, or often of several adjacent and distinct compounds. Each wife had her unmarried children living with her in her hut and the husband would move from one of his wives' huts to another's in strict regularity. A man who stayed for more than one night with one than with another ran the risk of causing quarreling between them. The fact that there is a term of abuse for a favorite wife showed me how real this jealousy can be. It contrasted very vividly with the apparent lack of jealousy felt by lovers who jilted one another. They felt not so much distress as anger for loss of pride or face. Compounds were grouped into clusters whose members recognized themselves as being members of a very small close-knit group under the authority of a single elder man. The number of compounds in such a group varied from four to twenty or more, but they all had a similar structure. In the anthropological literature this group is referred to as a joint or extended family, and seems to be particularly well suited to conditions of small-scale farming. I found that in Lugbara this local group was sometimes less than a joint family and sometimes consisted of five or six joint families, so I began to think of it as a family cluster, a term that gives a better idea of the actuality on the ground. Each family was based upon the men of a small lineage. The head of this lineage, the genealogically senior man in it, was called by the Lugbara a "big man"; I called him the Elder. He had control and authority over all members of his family cluster. This group had its own particular name, used both for the people and also for their territory. Once I had realized the nature of this group, by collecting details from large numbers of them throughout the area around me, then the whole system began to take shape. Traditionally there were no people with higher authority than the Elders of these tiny units, except for rainmakers and certain influential and wealthy men who could attract a following for their lifetimes without the position becoming hereditary.

The problem that faced me at this point therefore was to comprehend the means by which the Lugbara linked these many small family clusters into some coherent system. I could usually, though not always, tell the family clusters if I stood on a hill and looked down across the countryside, because although the boundaries were not very clearly marked there was usually a greater space of fields and unused land between them than there was between their constituent compounds. My first task was to understand the internal composition of these units. I did this by writing down large numbers of genealogies on which I could place all the members of a given cluster. Although they varied in size there was always a similar underlying organization. At the head was the Elder, typically an oldish man and usually with more than one wife. He might be alone in his generation or might have one or two younger brothers waiting to succeed him. Around his homestead were those of his sons and of his brothers' sons, all of whom in Lugbara kinship terminology were addressed by him merely as his "sons." All the men in his generation would refer to him as "father" and use the same term of address to any of his brothers. This is, of course, a widespread form of terminology and was not difficult for me to comprehend once I realized its general principles. I found that there was never any doubt in anyone's mind as to who was the true "father"; as Lugbara said, their use of the term refers largely to the fact that "fathers," as senior men, have authority over all their juniors. In fact, I realized increasingly that Lugbara, despite what seemed to me at the time to be their excessive social fragmentation and at times near-anarchy, were always very conscious of small nuances of authority and realized that it lay at the very heart of their social organization. They would talk with me about authority largely in terms of genealogical relationships, which were clearly among other things statements about relations of authority; so that the collection of genealogies became more significant the longer I was so occupied.

Genealogies

I have put down some of the details about local organization to indicate what I had learnt about it after three or four months. Although it sounds very obvious and would seem very easy information to get, in fact it took far more time and work than might at first appear likely. One difficulty was that when walking from one compound to another the social boundaries between them were not necessarily reflected in terms of actual territorial boundaries—although as I have mentioned I could often see them if I could find a small hill on which to stand to look out across the countryside. Another was that the Lugbara use only very few words to refer to the various territorial and descent groups that I found it imperative to distinguish very clearly. These were *aku* and *'buru*, a compound or homestead, of whatever size and internal composition; and *suru* and *ori'ba*, both of which refer to descent and territorial groups of any span from the smallest to the largest possible. I will mention these in detail later, but need say here that my lack of clear understanding about them weakened my everyday work for some months—yet without these months of drudgery I could never have comprehended their various significances.

I therefore decided that I had to begin by mapping the layout of compounds over a reasonably small area and then to put down the genealogies of all the people who lived in them. I chose two areas, one on either side of where I lived, mapped them and wrote down their genealogies until the people themselves told me that I had covered all the members of the two major sections (as I came later to refer to them although at the time I was uncertain as to their exact place in the wider system). Each had a population of some six or seven hundred people and the work took me about a month—although not full time. The mapping was extremely rough and resulted merely in two sketch maps with approximate distances between compounds and the main topographical features that seemed to have ecological and social significance for my informants. I also collected the two immense genealogies concerned. This may sound simple, but I think I almost never found a case in which the precise relationship between compounds, let alone their internal composition, were told to me without some objection or argument on the part of some of the bystanders.

The Lugbara themselves were always interested by all this and would sit with me for many hours to be sure that I wrote down the genealogies of these small groups correctly. I soon learned that there were certain dangers in this, because the genealogies were not written by Lugbara themselves and they would change over time, and also people of the same group would give me different versions of the same genealogy. At first I found this confusing and even annoying, and then realized that there must be some reason for it. To write down the genealogy of a family cluster would sometimes take me several hours. I would start by asking one man with whom I was talking for the names of his brothers, the name of his father, the names of his father's brothers, of his grandfather, of his grandfather's brothers, and so on. This was usually easy enough. I would then ask for the names of the wives of all these men and from where they had come. This was usually not difficult except in the cases of wives who had been divorced and returned to their natal homes. I realized very soon, as one might expect, that the names of girls born to the family cluster seemed to be very few. Since girls marry at the age of twelve or thirteen and go to live with their husbands five or ten miles away, their names would soon be forgotten in later generations. In addition, since women have lower status than men in terms of lineage responsibility, men would frequently say that I was wasting my time in writing down the names of women. When I would ask for the names of members of the group in this way, the names of attached men—sisters' sons, sisters' husbands, and clients, who might be living in the family cluster although of a different lineage ancestry —would frequently be omitted. I had therefore always first to draw a sketch map of the compounds of the cluster to make sure that no one was left out. Again the Lugbara would ask me why I wished to include such unimportant strangers, who not being of the core lineage were not regarded as of central importance.

Whatever the difficulties in collecting the genealogies I found it an essential task. Throughout the remainder of my fieldwork I always began any discussion in a new area—whether a sub-tribe, a major section, or a family cluster—by putting down the people with whom I was concerned in a genealogical framework. After a while I grew increasingly competent at this kind of recording and it took less time than during my first tentative attempts. I worked out forms of shorthand for kinship relationships, and found means of writing down large genealogies on several pages of a small notebook, and would then copy them onto larger sheets of paper after my return home in the evening (I found rolls of wrapping paper from the local store in Aru to be the best for this purpose). This kind of initial positioning of roles on the co-ordinates of descent, sex, generation, and age is essential in the study of a people such as the Lugbara, and I think probably of any other society too, including our own; the fact that non-anthropologists rarely do so is a weakness of their methods and not one of the genealogical method itself.

This work had a further advantage in that it was something that the

Lugbara saw immediately to be important and meaningful. I found that the writing down of a genealogy might take many hours, as I have said; but this was partly because I would be given a history of the group concerned as I did so. The people saw no point in merely reciting genealogical links: they were interested in the content of those links, in the sense of the actual historical roles played by the individuals whose names I was writing down. This was valuable both as history but also as indicating what were the areas of social importance in the system—where were the typical areas of tension and conflict, what were the processes of lineage and family development, what was the content of interpersonal relations, and so on. For example, I often found that two branches of a lineage had quarreled, by being told that two particular men had had a longstanding dispute and then had led their respective segments into the process of segmentation; later, when discussing the genealogical relationship of their respective grandparents I would find the ostensible reason for that quarrel, in a dispute over a bridewealth payment given for a long-past marriage. Or I would be told that a man whom I was placing in a genealogy had been regarded as a witch; again the accusations between him and his kin of the same generation could be traced back to a dispute several generations previously. In brief, by writing down genealogies I was forced to see the processes of group development over time; and this was particularly so when I was given variant versions of the same genealogy, the variants reflecting quarrels and stages in lineage segmentation.

I should say something here about the collection of kinship terms. Like all anthropologists I had been taught that the key to understanding any society and particularly societies of this kind is their system of kinship. As soon as I started to collect genealogies I started also to collect kinship terms, for obvious reasons. I began in a very naive manner by asking people how they referred to and how they addressed the various people whose names appeared in the genealogies of the various lineages of my acquaintance. After a short time I was able to construct with great satisfaction a chart of kinship terms of the kind I was used to seeing in the books I had read as a student. During these months I filled in many notes which covered the ideal behavior between kinsmen in the various categories. As time went on I began to notice discrepancies in my notes on the kinship system. I use the term "system" here advisedly since it is the usual term, but it seems to me somewhat inapposite. I noticed that several people told me that they addressed a certain person by a term that was incorrect according to my kinship tables. When I asked about this I was told that I was right to have noticed the discrepancy since people could change their kin relationship during the course of their lifetimes. People told me also that it often happens that one may address a person by two terms, each of which is suitable for a given occasion. At first I assumed that this was a perfectly natural outcome of certain types of marriage within a given social group, so that two people could be related to each other in succeeding generations in more than one way and so by more than one term. I then noticed, when watching the events that composed the process of sacrifice to the dead, that one of the functions of sacrifice was to reorder the pattern of genealogical relationships within a lineage. The basic principle was the simple one that when a man dies his kinship position is filled in certain situations and for certain purposes by his successor. So that in this way a man whose father had just died would in some everyday situations continue to call his father's brother by the term for "father" as he had always done, but in other situations he might address him as "brother" and be addressed by him by the same term. In these latter situations all the other members of his lineage would have to adjust the terms by which they addressed him. Another common situation was when a member of a lineage who was known as "sister's son" by the core members of the group, because his grandfather or great-grandfather came to live with their grandfathers as a sister's son, changed his relationship from "sister's son" to "brother." This would happen also in the case of people who were living as clients with a host lineage and who therefore lacked any formal lineage link with their hosts. If the relationship between them and their hosts were personally very close and if it were clear that their sense of loyalty to the interests of the host lineage were greater than that to their real lineage kin living elsewhere, then it would be decided on the occasion of a sacrifice that the formerly held genealogies were wrong and in reality their ancestors had been true members of the group, so that they became "brothers." This would not mean that all the members of the lineage would happily accept them as brothers; there would often be various anomalies of address so that, for example, a man would sometimes call them his brothers and sometimes call them his sisters' sons; it would depend on whether they were talking about marriage, cattle, or sacrifice.

The point I am trying to make here is again a simple but important one. It is that I found very soon that although my earlier training had been essential to me, it was very easy to be overwhelmed by it and to be led by it into ways of patterning the information that I gathered, so that if my information fitted the expected pattern I would be satisfied by it and not see its true significance for the people themselves. Kinship is an idiom by which various relations between people, that are significant in a certain situation, can easily be expressed, can be given an emotive content and sanction, and can be fitted together into a single system of relations. For Lugbara, at any rate, there is really no such thing as a kinship system in the same sense as a political or economic system. They perform activities that are economic or political, but there are no activities that may be called kinship ones. Lugbara adapt the terms of kinship to a given situation without any apparent sense of conflict or incongruity. What I am saying as far as fieldwork method is concerned is that it is not good enough merely to collect genealogies and lists of kinship terms that are divorced from a given social situation, but that one must analyze the situation itself and then see in what ways the genealogies and kin terms are actually used. I found this difficult at first because I had assumed, as do many of those who construct elaborate comparative models of kinship systems, that these terms are in fact elements of systems in their own right. Such a naive assumption becomes misleading and incorrect in an actual social situation.

Myth

Although everyone with whom I spoke about his genealogy would usually tell me a different story, I was always told the same set of myths. Often younger men would relate the genealogy of their lineage to me but when I asked about the origins of their society would tell me to ask their seniors who were the people to know about things of this kind. These were the myths of the Lugbara, which are told by the elder men as a means of explaining the universe, the nature of the world and the place of man within it, and the nature and activities of Divinity.

I found that the genealogy of any lineage always went back to one of the two hero-ancestors, as I call them, Dribidu and Jaki. They were not the first men on earth but were the founders of Lugbara society in the form it has today (according to Lugbara statement; obviously we may assume that historically their society has always been slowly changing, but that is another matter). Before the time of the heroes, using our own concept of time stretching back to the beginning of the world, there were other people who had been put in the world by the Creator Spirit. Lugbara told me that in the beginning the Creator put a man and a woman on the world in a place somewhere in the Sudan, outside their present homeland. This man and woman were not true brother and sister, nor were they husband and wife. They were simply there. In the myth the woman was created pregnant and gave birth to wild animals and then to a son and daughter. The son and daughter committed incest and the daughter bore in her turn a son and daughter. This went on for several generations until the myth states in a somewhat undecided manner the birth of the two heroes I have mentioned above. On other occasions Lugbara would tell me a different myth about the origin of the world; that there was a time that men and women could move to and from the sky by means of a rope, a tree, or some kind of tower. One day this fell down and the people were scattered over the face of the world, each speaking their own language and the descendants of each forming the tribes of the world today.

I have published accounts of these myths elsewhere and need not do so here. What I want to say is something of the way Lugbara related these myths to me. Obviously, as soon as I heard them I realized I was hearing myths of a kind that are widespread if not universal but I had never realized their significance for the people who told them. They believed them, but did not relate them as though history in our sense of the term. It was no good my asking which of the people in the first myth were those who went to and from the sky. Lugbara simply said that they did not know and that I was asking a stupid question. And of course they were right. They were trying to say two things with these myths. They were telling me how men came to inhabit the earth and they were answering the important question of why if Divine Spirit created men he then chose to go away from them and live in the sky. These two questions are universal, of interest to every society in the world. And many peoples, perhaps most peoples, answer them in remarkably similar ways. The other main corpus of myths dealt with the doings of the two hero-ancestors. The myths about each one were told to me in similar terms. Again, I have described them elsewhere and need only mention here a few salient points. Each of the two heroes lived outside Lugbaraland with his children and his sister's son. It was no good my asking what might seem an obvious question, that is, who were their wives and who were the husbands of their sisters. These details were seen as irrelevant to the point of the myth and Lugbara simply said they did not know. They added, quite courteously so as to help me learn about such matters, that to have asked these questions showed my ignorance and lack of comprehension. And again they were right. They realized, although without the words with which to express it explicitly, that to understand their culture I would have to learn to think in mythopoeic terms: literal or historiographical concepts were not sufficient. I would have to learn to accept their myths in the same way that they themselves did, and not regard them merely as material for my notebook.

One of the myths, that of Dribidu, tells that every day he and one of his sons would go hunting and every day he would return alone with liver meat. He said that this was from a buffalo that he had killed, but in the hunting his son had unfortunately first been killed by the buffalo. This happened day after day until finally everyone became suspicious of his story. Again it was quite pointless for me to ask who were the other people in the story. The teller would exclaim, somewhat peevishly, that as he had not been there he could not possibly know. One day Dribidu was secretly followed on his hunt and was seen to kill his son, take out his liver and bring it back with him. At this he was driven out and left his homeland with his sister's son and one bull, crossed the River Nile and came into the present Lugbaraland. When they came to Lugbara they climbed up Mount Eti. There they hunted and killed a buffalo, but had no fire on which to cook its meat. The sister's son scanned the country beneath them and on the horizon saw fire. Dribidu sent him to see what the fire was and he returned to say that there was a leper woman living in poverty with a fire but no food to cook on it. Hastily they took their meat to the fire, cooked it and shared it with the leper woman. Dribidu healed her with magical medicines and stayed there with her. She became pregnant by him. Her brothers then appeared with spears and after a fight made Dribidu pay bridewealth to marry her. The woman bore him a son, who was the founder of one of the clans of today. Dribidu did the same with many leper women in various parts of the country. The home of each woman became the homeland of each particular clan, and the descendants of their sons, who intermarried with one another's sisters, form the Lugbara people of today. Dribidu finally died, and his grave was shown to me on the top of Mount Eti. A similar tale was told to me on many occasions about the other hero-ancestor, who is reputed to be buried on the other mountain, Liru. The members of a particular clan told the same myth with their own clan founder cast in the role of a son of the particular leper woman ancestress.

Once again, it was pointless to ask for details of the other persons in these myths. They are irrelevant and Lugbara did not concern themselves with them. Yet myths are vastly important, since by them Lugbara explain a great many things of their present-day society: the coming of their ancestors to their present habitat; the beginnings of settlement, marriage, and feuding; the position of wives as dependents of their husbands; the change from hunting to farming; the nature of sexual relationships; and the nature of kinship—the principle of organization that is the heart of their society. These myths are not folktales: I realized that since they had motifs that I knew were found in tales of peoples other than the Lugbara, it might be interesting to work out their distribution and diffusion in the southern Sudan culture area and beyond. But it was more exciting and also I think far more valuable to analyze them as statements about social relations that the Lugbara saw as being so important that they had to be stated symbolically and mythopoeically.

When people would tell me these myths, they would act them out dramatically with gestures and much walking up and down while speaking, and there is not the least doubt that they firmly believed them. However I found it not easy to know what constituted this belief. I never knew whether Lugbara believed that Dribidu and Jaki literally existed, although I was certainly shown what were said to be their graves—which were actual grave sites, with remains of huts and potsheads nearby. I can only say that they believed in their historical actuality in the way that we believe in the actuality of, for example, an Old Testament prophet: we do not know what he looked like, nor do we consider it very important, although we can ponder on what kind of man he must or might have been and what were his motives in his relations with others. The men with me, who were mostly young and who had experienced the outside world and realized that some of their former beliefs had been ill founded (they had, for example, seen poor Indians while in the army, and so had their views of Indian traders changed considerably), certainly seemed to believe in their existence, and they certainly understood their significance for the comprehension of their world. This was clearly at the heart of the matter.

I can explain this more concisely if I relate briefly another myth. When I asked Lugbara to tell me about the setting up of colonial rule, I was told that the first Europeans came to the country walking upside-down; and older people have told me that in my own country, on the other side of Lake Albert, this is indeed the way we behave there today. The first Europeans came in this way, but as soon as they realized that they were being looked at they righted themselves and then walked on their feet. The first Englishman, A. E. Weatherhead, was said to have had powers that could have only been described as miraculous. He could walk across the country mysteriously at fantastic speeds and had spiritual powers that quite overawed the Lugbara. Since his day the various Europeans in the area have been ordinary people, and it is thought that many are the descendants of the earlier Europeans among them. Now the main difference between the myths of the heroes and the Europeans is that in our sense the one occurred at the beginning of the world and the other occurred between 1895 and 1914, within living memory. The man who first told me about the Europeans in any detail was my cook's father, who had himself worked as a servant for the first Belgian administrator in 1900. He would tell me of their everyday activities, saying that they were in fact quite pleasant men although they had some unusual habits: they ate strange foods and consumed enormous quantities of gin and tea. But he would always repeat emphatically that they walked upside-down and had miraculous powers. And this was confirmed by other men who had actually been present when the Belgians first appeared. At first I could not understand what was being said to me: I tried to work out a "correct" version of these stories, then wondered whether I was not hearing the relics of distant tales of medieval giants and the like. But finally I realized that when the old men used this particular idiom they were doing so for a definite purpose—although not perhaps a self-conscious one: they were trying to tell me that these were people who came into their society from the outside world. I looked again at the myth of first creation and of the hero-ancestors and realized that the same idiom was being used there. The people, the personages of the myth before the hero-ancestors, the brothers and sisters who committed incest, were also "upside-down," although their inversion was moral rather than physical. That is, they committed incest and cannibalism, the very negation of socially responsible behavior toward one's own kin.

The reason for my friends' insistence on telling me these myths, which were related to me on dozens of separate occasions by many different people—and their insisting that I write them down, once they had realized that I wrote down the information that I regarded as important—was made clear to me when one old man explained, quite correctly, that I could not possibly understand the landscape spread out before me until I had learned of the travels of the heroes. I could see before me the miles of homesteads and cultivated country, with the great burial trees scattered across it (the trees left to grow on the graves of genealogically important men, which therefore acted as a kind of record of lineage movement in the past), and in the distance the twin peaks of Mounts Eti and Liru rising from the haze: the myths made sense of it all. I had concentrated first, as I think I had to do, on what seemed then to be the basic matters of technology, farming, and homestead organization; but the Lugbara soon took charge of my learning and taught me the things that they considered essential if I were to understand the life around me. These myths are at the basis of all Lugbara culture, its basic symbolic statements, and once I had a rudimentary knowledge of the technical, the Lugbara saw to it that I turned to the more symbolic, the essence of what was meant by "Lugbara."

In telling me, at least by implication, that I should not understand the organization of their society unless I first comprehended its basic principles and cosmological notions, the Lugbara were far more correct and sophisticated than I realized at the time. A social structure is not, after all, an object that is directly observable in any objective sense; one cannot count or measure it. It is an abstraction, used by the people themselves to comprehend relations of power and authority. To understand the particular way in which any given people do this necessitates that the observer tries, as best as he can, to see the pattern of relations of power and authority as do the people he is studying. If he assumes that he can do otherwise, then he is merely assuming that the society he is observing is a variation or aberration of his own; and that will not get anyone very far. I was shown—although it took me many months to realize it—that the Lugbara were making statements to me, as they made to themselves, of the nature and distribution of power and authority; those about power were made in terms of myth, those about authority were made in terms of genealogy. This taught me another lesson: although I was ready to learn about the various aspects of Lugbara society independently of each other—economy, political organization, religion, and so on—in fact they were not distinct, or more accurately, the relations between these aspects that seemed proper to me were not those that necessarily seemed proper to the Lugbara. They would speak of what I would think of as "politics" by telling me of myths; they would tell me of topography by telling me cosmologies, and so on. When I saw this I had learnt something that opened the doors to their culture to me in a way that I had not imagined possible.

Clans and Lineages

It soon became clear that the Lugbara conceived of their local organization as one based on clans and lineages, each of which consisted of groups of patrilineal kinsmen and kinswomen. There is no point here in presenting the various pieces of information that I was to put together to form a system. But it is worth trying to show something of the confusion that I felt when confronted with a system such as this and the lines of approach that I followed, some of which proved to be correct while others were blind alleys.

I have said that I started this work by collecting the genealogies of people whom I met in the course of my everyday visiting. This soon led the Lugbara to assume that this was my primary interest and one or two Lugbara who had been to school announced that I was studying something known as "history." There is no translation for this word in Lugbara and it was adopted into the local language as referring to my activity of asking about genealogy and writing the replies on pieces of paper. The Lugbara understood perfectly well what I was doing, because after all it was something that they did themselves all the time; but they did not write down genealogies on pieces of paper, and their acceptance of my genealogical interest meant that they also accepted my practice of writing in a notebook, and took little further notice of it. They were perfectly aware of the importance of kinship ties between the living, between the living and the dead, and between the dead themselves. These relationships are statements about such matters as the exercise of authority and power, the inheritance of rights in land and cattle, and succession to office. They themselves talked in this idiom and so found it perfectly meaningful that I should try to understand the details of it. There was another aspect of their interest in this study of mine. They had come across one or two other Europeans who had shown interest in their traditional customs and had written down information in notebooks. These had been either missionaries who wished to destroy these customs or administrative officers collecting information for use in court cases. But none of them had ever done what I was doing, which was to show interest in what was to them the basic idiom of social life. It was here of course that my training as an anthropologist was significant, and I think my very interest in these matters, together with my explanation that I was a teacher who wished to understand them in order to teach people in Europe about them made them less suspicious of my motives. I think it fair to say that my explanation was at least honest and in fact no harm ever came to them from the fact that they told me about these matters.

As I have said, Lugbara tried to explain what may be called their social topography by telling me about their myths of origin. Since all these myths when related to me ended with statements such as "and that son of that leper woman was the founder of such-and-such a clan," it seemed to be obvious for me to try and understand the system of clans. The word for clan and lineage in Lugbara is *suru*. So I started collecting the names of clans and lineages. I am not quite sure now what I intended to do with my list of clan-names, but I am glad that I tried to make one. I collected the clan-names of every *suru* wherever I went, and attempted to find some indication of where the various clan homelands were in the vast area spread out like a map before my eyes. In other words, I started to collect information of the kind that had earlier been collected in other areas by ethnologists interested in clan diffusion and historical reconstructions. This is not to say that I did then, or do now, think that such work was in any way mistaken or inadequate; it is merely that I realized that my interests were in fact different, as in fact were those of the Lugbara themselves, and that I would have to rethink the whole situation and change my aims and tactics. Contrary to my expectations there emerged no consistent pattern of clan distribution from the tables that I so laboriously collected. There were several dozen names of clans that reappeared in every locality with an apparently quite haphazard distribution. Some of the names were translatable and fell into certain categories: they referred to topographical features, to ancestry, to ridicule or opprobrium, or had no obvious meaning at all. I was later to realize, as I did when I collected lists of personal names, that these categories were in fact to give me several leads as to the basic values of Lugbara cosmological categorization. But at the time I was after something else.

It was apparent that I was on the wrong track and that I would have to tackle this problem in a rather more sophisticated manner. I found that the word *suru* was used for several kinds of grouping. Some of these were true clans and lineages according to the usual anthropological usage, others were territorial areas and groupings; I could deal with this one easily since I had read *The Nuer* several times as a student. But the size of the *suru* also varied considerably, as did its place in what was obviously a system of segmentary descent groups. I then discovered that the smaller of these groups were referred to by another term, *ori'ba*, which meant literally "ghost-people"; and then I discovered a third term, *enyati* ("eaters"). The problem was therefore to find out exactly what these groups were and how they fitted together into a single system. I found that this was always the first essential piece of information to be collected whenever I went to a new part of the country. The Lugbara found it difficult to get me to understand the system in a way satisfactory to them. They showed me that I was still not on the right track by analyzing the system in any local area in terms of "big" and "little" *suru* and *ori'ba*. They could conceptualize the system in the terms in which they realized that I saw it; but it dawned upon me fairly soon that this was not the way in which they conceived it themselves.

I therefore changed my tactics from trying to work out the paradigm of lineage organization and began asking questions about the functions and activities associated with the local and descent groups. The reason was of course simple, in that I could in this way discover more about the ways in which the people themselves regarded these groups. They began to discuss lineages and clans in two main frames of reference. I had begun my queries by filling in genealogies, and in my Western way of thinking I would start by asking the name of a man's father and grandfather and going back to the earliest ancestors on earth. But after a little I realized that the Lugbara defined clans and lineages in different ways: they defined clans by reference to their founding ancestors, whereas they defined lineages in terms of the actual distribution on the ground of the people who were members at the present time. In other words, clans were defined by reference to myth, and lineages by reference to the experience of living people. They were both units in a single system but their functions were distinct. Lugbara conceived of clans as being permanent, as unchanging elements in a world of continual petty change throughout the lifetime of any living person. The everyday distribution of people across the landscape is continually changing as people are born, grow up, marry, have children, and in their turn die. As they proceed through their lives, they are born into, attach themselves to, and are members of lineages of various spans. They always remain full members of their natal lineages but are attached in varying ways to other lineages: if wives, they move to the lineage homes of their husbands, and many men choose for one reason or another to live in the territory of lineages other than their own. Also, and this is perhaps more important, lineages are continually changing in size according to variations in birth and death rates; in the past they were always moving across the countryside in search of new land; and are in a continual process of segmentation in order to accommodate the variations in demographic factors and in the carrying capacity of a given piece of land. These characteristics are of course those of the units in any segmentary lineage system, and I need say no more about them here. By contrast clans are regarded as permanent and give the Lugbara a pattern of order and regularity in terms of which they can conceive their own society and its neighbors.

When I asked Lugbara about the functions of these various groups they began to talk in terms of feud and warfare, of intermarriage, of sacrifices, and of the various conflicts and disputes that led to violence and sacrifice and which in time culminated in the splitting of lineages into their constituent segments. Traditionally the Lugbara jural system was based on the recognized and formal sanctions of feud and warfare. They lacked kings, chiefs and police, so that organized self-help was the main sanction between groups. Within the small groups themselves the main sanctions were and still are the use of various religious processes, such as the invocation of the dead and accusations of witchcraft and sorcery. I soon discovered that people quarreled mainly on account of the sharing of land and particularly about the distribution of the irrigable plots along the stream beds; and they quarreled over women, over the sharing of bridewealth to get new wives, over the behavior of wives once married and over the rights in their children. Of course since it is wives who used the irrigable land and who could only be married by the giving of cattle, the distribution of women, of land, and of cattle were all very closely linked. Since one could not marry one's kinswomen it follows that the relationship of affines was that of unrelated men who lack ancestors in common. They could not observe mutual good behavior as part of their duty to common ancestors, and the only recourse open to them was that of fighting. The last outbreaks of warfare were probably about 1930, but I found that all Lugbara men who had been more than about fifteen years old in the 1930s could tell me about the operation of feud and warfare. I had hoped at first that they would tell me about them in terms of the lineage paradigm that I had roughly constructed from the genealogies that I so laboriously collected, but that simply did not work. The only way was to ask for details of actual cases of feud and warfare that the men concerned had taken part in or at least could remember with fair accuracy. I found, not unnaturally, that they tended to exaggerate the glories of the deeds of prowess of themselves and their lineage kin—Lugbara can never be accused of false modesty. What was at first told to me as a glorious war which seemed to involve the entire countryside for months at a time usually turned out after detailed questioning to have involved a dozen men on each side who had fought sporadically for a week or two. But this very exaggeration showed me something of the importance of fighting for the Lugbara and of the central part that it played in the traditional political system.

More important, I soon found that I was asking questions that, although they could be answered in terms of giving names of particular lineages taking part in a particular feud, were answered among the Lugbara themselves in quite other terms. They did not use the words for clan and lineage nor did they always use the names of these groups, but instead used terms that referred to categories of kin and clusters of groupings that were defined according to a particular situation. I have described these categories elsewhere and there is no need to say much about them here. They are the terms that mean "clansmen," "non-clansmen," "mother's brother's people," and "wife's brother's people"; these terms refer in a shorthand way to whatever constellation of kin groups happens to be relevant in any given situation. It is assumed that one's listeners know who are the clansmen or mother's people to whom one is referring at a particular moment. By this means one can make sense and consistency out of a situation of which the pattern is very fluid and in fact may change from one occasion to another.

An Elder of Maraca, in northern Lugbaraland. He was a young married man when the first Belgians came in 1900, and so was about seventy years old when this photograph was taken.

My collection of genealogies and clan names did however have one valuable consequence. I realized that when a lineage splits into two or more segments as a consequence of land pressure or persistent quarreling, the new segments are given names that are the lineage names of the women who were the co-wives of the original lineage founder. That is, if a great-grandfather had three wives, when his descendants decided to split they would break into three segments, each of which would see its unity in terms of its descent from one of those wives. The new segment took the name of that woman's natal lineage. This was the explanation for the repetition of the same clan names across the countryside that I had found so confusing and for which I could find no apparent pattern of distribution. The points that I am making are, of course, that I discovered that I was investigating processes of lineage and group development and not a static distribution of people and groups—like the Lugbara themselves I regarded a society as something fairly stable but came to see that any society is always in a continuing condition of change and growth; and that I could only understand these processes by the laborious collection of case-histories, and not merely by asking my informants for vague principles of organization that they themselves took for granted and so could not easily explain to me in conventional anthropological terms.

The Wider Culture Area

Once I had acquired some idea of the structure of everyday life in the area in which I had been living, I realized that I should visit other parts of the country in order to discover the main differences between one part of Lugbaraland and another. My difficulty was that I had no idea as to the main cultural divisions of the total society, so I decided on the obvious course of visiting parts of the country that were at least a good many miles away from that area with which I had become familiar. I therefore devoted a few weeks to traveling around the few main roads that crossed the district and in that time visited very briefly not only some other parts of Lugbaraland but also just entered the areas occupied by neighboring tribal groupings.

It was both confusing and enlightening to realize the diversity of culture in different parts of the countryside. Although I had not thought about it in great detail, I had expected to find a uniformity of culture throughout Lugbaraland. The more I traveled through the country, however, the more I became aware of the remarkable diversity of elements of material culture, and, as I was to discover later, of cultural behavior and belief as well. I soon noticed that every few miles there were slight differences in such things as the markings tattooed on bodies, the ways of thatching huts and granaries, the shapes and sizes of pots and calabashes, the patterning of spears and arrows, and perhaps most of all in the shapes and sizes of shrines and in the places these shrines were built. In addition, each part of the country seemed to have its own style of life, and although much of this variation was due to differences in the landscape itself and the types of crops grown, after I had had more experience of the society I became aware that these differences were essentially those of the composition of population and settlement as well as variations in size of local clusters of homesteads. Underlying this, there was of course a general uniformity of culture that could be called "Lugbara."

I spent two more weeks staying for a few days at a time in some areas on the borders of Lugbaraland. I spent a few days among the southern Madi near Rhino Camp and a few days among the northern Madi, both in the highlands west of the Nile and in the low country to the east of that river. I had already spent a day or two with another anthropologist who was then working among the Acholi, some hundred miles to the east of the Lugbara, on the east of the Nile. I spent some days among the north-eastern Lugbara of Aringa, who were clearly affected by their proximity to the Sudan and to the Muslim-affected cultures of that region. I spent a day or two among the Kakwa to the north and also travelled to Kajo-Kaji in Kuku country, in the Sudan. I visited the Lugbara living in the adjacent districts of the Congo; and I later returned there for a few weeks to stay at the headquarters of a chief who was the cousin of one of the Uganda chiefs who had become a friend of mine. A few months later I had the opportunity to spend another week in the Congo driving as far as the countries of the Azande and Mangbetu, crossing the lands occupied by the Keliko and Logo; and likewise I went to the southwest through the country of the Alur into the areas occupied by the Ndu (Okebu) and 'Bale (Lendu).

These journeys were valuable for two reasons. One was the obvious one of having a few days' change of scene, and the other was the more important one of getting a sense of the wider cultural area in which Lugbara is situated. A society like the Lugbara is in no way a discrete and clearly defined cultural or political unit, and I found that there were cultural differences within the Lugbara that were as great as those existing between them and some of their neighbors. I soon observed the significance of the fact that the Lugbara and Madi were the most southeasterly members of a congeries of closely related peoples that extend to the northwest at least as far as the Azande. I knew this already from having read Tucker's *Grammar of the Eastern Sudanic Languages*, but actually to see this on the ground was an eye-opener for me. Thereafter whenever I heard Lugbara talking about their myths of origin and their migrations from the north and west I was able to conceive the world to some extent as they did themselves. I realized that the concept of culture area is a far more meaningful one than I had previously thought and that I had chosen a people who were at the very southeasterly edge of such an area. This realization enabled me at least to be aware of the possibility of influence from the cultures of their Nilotic and other neighbors who were in their own turn on the edges of other culture areas. In brief these short journeys enabled me to put the Lugbara into a wider system in both space and time. A final point of value in these journeys lay in the comments by those Lugbara who went along with me. The comments focused in all cases on the differences in the landscapes and in the consequent differences in conceiving the social topography of those peoples. The main distinction they made was between their own high and open countryside and the more enclosed and more thickly wooded area to the east. In the west the vast plains of Keliko are but sparsely treed and occupied, and this was in its own way another vivid contrast to the crowded Lugbara landscape with which I had grown so familiar.

5

The Study of Religion

I HAD EARLY REALIZED that the Lugbara, although at first sight hardly a very religious people, discussed matters and concepts that we would call "religious" in a great many situations that we would not speak of as being so. This is not to imply that they are "religious" in their thinking and that Westerners are not so (whatever those phrases may mean), but rather that to the Lugbara the spheres of what we might regard as the natural and supernatural are not distinct but are rather parts of a single whole. To many Christians and others of the West there is no barrier between the natural and the supernatural, or what may be called the everyday and the religious and spiritual. But I am writing here of my own opinions and beliefs, which whether right or wrong in any ultimate sense do make this distinction. I say this deliberately, because it is sometimes said that I or any other Westerner, who as a member of Western society accepts general and often unthought-out Christian beliefs, cannot really understand the religious beliefs of another culture. I do not think that this is true. I myself have one wife, not four, yet I think that I can understand what it is like to be a husband who has four wives, as did many of the men I knew in Lugbaraland. In the same way I am able to accept a religion other than my own, even though I do not believe its tenets.

I have already related something of the importance the Lugbara attach to their mythology; and I realized that making sacrifices and dealing with the effects of magic took up a great part of the life of any adult man. Women and children were not so concerned with ritual matters, and tended on the whole to disregard them. I think it is best for me to describe my growing understanding of Lugbara religion by dividing the narrative into three sections: the various rituals that I saw performed; magic, witchcraft, and sorcery; and the various manifestations of Christianity that were in vogue during my stay. In fact, my knowledge of these three main aspects of their religion developed concurrently. But an attempt to show in detail, and chronologically, how I acquired an understanding of ritual would be so confusing as to make it almost meaningless. When I read my field notes today I am amused to see my ignorance of religious matters during most of

46

the first year of my stay. I think the main reason, apart from my lack of knowledge of the language, was my lack of comprehension of the role played by religion in Lugbara life. At first I collected from informants as many accounts as I could of their religious beliefs and of the ways in which they performed rituals, and I wrote down daily descriptions of what I observed. I have mentioned the great cultural diversity from one part of the country to another; this diversity is particularly noticeable in the field of religious practices. The consequence was that my notes contained an astonishing and confusing diversity of detail, and it was not until fairly late in my fieldwork that I could discern much pattern in what I was observing. The pattern in the events I witnessed was due to the social function played by them; so that it was not until I realized what this function was that I was able to make much sense of what I saw. I am perhaps implying, of course, that there is a single pattern that must first be understood before one can adequately collect field material, but that would be a false implication. One of the difficulties and paradoxes of anthropological fieldwork is that one cannot really understand what one is observing unless he sees every detail as an element in a structure, but this structure cannot be discerned until most of the elements have been collected. To have the structure or pattern complete with every detail in place would appear in fact to be an impossibility. The reason is obvious: no society is totally unchanging, so that there are always discrepancies and contradictions of detail in the organization of social life. What the fieldworker does in essence is to build up hypothetical structures or patterns as he goes along. Every new fact that he gathers can either be fitted into that structure, or if not, he is forced to change the structure. I return here to the point made at the beginning of this book: One cannot order one's field research according to a set program, but must be led by the nature of the culture one is observing along a path which may lead very far from one's original aims and hypotheses.

Burial of the Dead

My first notes on what may loosely be called Lugbara religion were made after I had visited a funeral; and although they may now seem to be very naive—and indeed they are so—it is worth my saying something about the way I described what I saw as an example of the way that I was slowly to learn about Lugbara religious practice and belief. I had walked one morning into Nyio to find one or two compounds crowded with visitors. There were many men standing in small groups, talking, arguing, and drinking beer. Elsewhere women were grinding grain and scurrying from one hut to another with baskets of food and pots of beer. The children were chattering everywhere. At first I might have stumbled upon an impromptu party, until I realized that in one compound two or three women were wailing, throwing dust and ashes upon themselves and rolling on the ashes of the fire of the previous evening. Outside the huts in the compound one or two men were tuning drums. The men glared at me and the women looked sullen and edged away. One or two of the men whom I already knew looked embarrassed and would like to have disclaimed acquaintance with me. Oguda told me that his father's brother had died that night and was to be buried that day. We went to see his father to offer our sympathy. He was already very drunk and once he saw that I was not to be put off, welcomed me profusely. I was given beer and introduced to the circle of men, most of whom were also excited and well filled with beer. I was told that inside one of the huts the body had been washed and was now wrapped in white cloth bought for the occasion, and outside the hut some men had dug a grave about five foot deep with a long recess at one side. After some waiting the body was taken out and lowered into the grave while the men of the immediate family stood around the grave watching. They then began to talk, clearly addressing the corpse as it lay beneath them, pointing at it and shouting angrily. My Lugbara was not good enough at that time to understand what they said, and since Oguda was by then somewhat unsteady in his speech I was not able to grasp the gist of their remarks. After twenty minutes or so the men began to fill in the grave and other men began to beat the three drums which had been tightened at the fire and were ready for play. I noticed that as soon as the dancing began small groups of men who had been standing together ran to the dance ground and danced in line holding spears and quivers. Soon another group entered the arena and took over the small dancing space. There was a good deal of argument and competition between the various groups, many of which had a second line of women. Occasionally a man and a woman would run to the edge of the ground and shout in a falsetto voice, then shoot an arrow into the bushland before returning to the dance ground. The dancing and shouting and singing were to continue all that evening until the moon went down soon after midnight.

I went home very dispirited, having seen what was clearly an event of some importance and interest but without having understood the least thing about it except that it was a funeral. The next morning there were some more dancing and singing at the same spot. But by the afternoon things had quieted and I was able to try to make some sense out of what I had seen. I sat down and tried to write a coherent account of the events. The main questions were those of the identity and the lineage and kinship relationships of the various people who had taken part. I realized that the people associated with the disposal of the body were sisters' sons of the dead man, and thus members of other lineages. The men who had stood around the grave were the men of the dead man's minimal lineage, and had indeed been cursing him and showing their "joy" that he was dead. It was only at a later date that I understood the significance of this. I was to realize that the groups of men and women who had gone to dance together each represented the members of a lineage related to the dead man in one way or another, and I was told that the dancing was to "rejoice." It became clear that I would need to know the answers to several questions. One was the significance of the lineage relationships concerned. Others were the significance of cursing the body, of rejoicing at a man's death, and obviously of various notions of death, life, and the soul of the person.

Here I am making certain points that I think are important in fieldwork. One is that although this funeral took place when I had been in the country for only a few weeks it was to be typical of many that I witnessed. I had always assumed that the fieldworker would sit with book in hand, asking clear and intelligent questions and making clear and intelligent notes. Perhaps there have been anthropologists who have worked in this way, but I rather doubt it: and if there have been, they must have worked rather too far from the hurly-burly of everyday life to have grasped much of the flavor of it. Toward the end of my stay I was perhaps to come nearer to that ideal, but it was to be at the stage when I was filling in specific points in situations of which I already knew the main structure. Also of course I was always able to take coherent notes when talking privately with informants. The difficulty was to do this when watching a disorderly and apparently chaotic scene such as that I had briefly described, and I have deliberately set down the superficial impression that I received at the time and that I had to use as a basis for further thought and investigation. Yet if I had not actually witnessed that and been confused by it, I would have missed its most important elements altogether. The important elements of course are those that the participants themselves take for granted, so that they are not always likely to remark upon them in a conversation; and since the fieldworker would be unaware of them he would be unlikely to ask about them. After visiting the funeral I realized how important were the collective emotions that were being expressed, which seemed to me to be out of place and unexpected; in our own culture we do not expect people to rejoice at death nor to shout abuse at a corpse. It was clear, therefore, that I did not understand the motives for the display of these emotions, and would also have to check very carefully whether or not I had in fact recognized them correctly. Later, when talking with people about these matters, I realized the obvious fact that they were unable to translate what I had seen into words that were adequate for my purpose. For example, it was clear that when people said they were "rejoicing," that the English word "rejoice" was not always adequate to translate the Lugbara term *aiikosi owu*. I was later to understand, after seeing many of these and similar occasions, that the Lugbara term refers not so much to joy in our sense, as to a satisfaction at recognizing and reordering a social relationship that had been broken by the death. The death causes a period of chaos and confusion. This is brought to an end when it is restructured, by the recognition of new ties of relationship between the various people and groups concerned. Such a remark, simple though it is, has a host of implications for the ways in which we see relations of kinship, lineage, and clan. So that again it became obvious to me that I could not get very far without an understanding of the basic social relationships that I have already mentioned in earlier sections.

In later weeks and months I was to see many funerals and death dances. I found that they always followed a similar pattern, although with variation in detail. At the same time I witnessed many other rituals and also talked with many people about the beliefs that they held about them. I asked people about the elements of man, the spirit and the soul and dissolution after death, the significance of the ancestors and ghosts and their relationship to living men and to Divine Spirit. I have described all these elsewhere and need not repeat the details here. But I should say one thing that seems to me to be important. At first I would plunge virtually at random into discussion of any kind of belief that came into my head. Bit by bit a pattern began to emerge from the details that I thus collected. I realized finally that there were one or two concepts that were key ones and that if I could adequately understand these then I could make some sense of the whole. These beliefs seemed to be arranged into a scheme that covered the entire universe and the place of man within it. In this scheme there were two main concepts: One was that of *adro* and the other that of *amve*. *Adro* means "spirit" and may refer both to the Creator God, to the immanent and evil aspect of the Divinity, and to the individual spirit within the individual body. The spirit in any aspect and any manifestation was said to be *amve* or "outside." It may be outside the world or outside the cultivated fields and homesteads, or metaphorically "outside" the responsible element of a person. If something is outside, there must be something else inside, and so I came to the pattern of complementary opposites that plays so central a part in Lugbara religious belief. Once I had realized the significance of this simple but all-pervasive dichotomy in Lugbara thought, much that I was to hear and witness fell into its proper place without difficulty. It might be argued that such a dualism is widespread throughout the world (as indeed it is) and so I should have recognized it immediately. But had I done that I would have fallen into the trap of regarding Lugbara behavior as an example of something I already expected to find. But in this research situation such deductive thinking would have been misleading and dangerous: anthropology is an inductive science and one must approach field experience in its own right. From it one may later adduce generalizations, not the other way about.

Rites of Sacrifice

I began also to attend other rites and in particular those involving sacrifice to the dead. I had noticed very early that almost every compound had one or two shrines, built of stone and set under the granaries and against the walls of the huts. Others were placed in the bushland and in the cattle compounds. There seemed to be a bewildering variety of them, although one or two types predominated. They did not seem to be particularly sacred objects, in that children, chickens, and goats wandered unconcernedly among them, but they were always swept and kept clean. I asked questions about them and soon collected a mass of information about their names and the various categories of ghost, ancestor, or spirit that occupied them. I learned that different people made different kinds of sacrifices at them, on different occasions and situations. But it was in fact some time before I actually witnessed and took part in sacrifices: There is no doubt that the Lugbara were uneasy about this until I had been there for several months. There were two main reasons for this suspicion. One was the obvious one that the missionaries, who were mostly Europeans, strongly disapproved of the cult of the dead and the beliefs associated with it. I was told on more than one occasion by missionaries that my attending rituals made their work all the harder. They did this in no unfriendly spirit and they were justified in saying what they did; on the other hand I think that in my position I was justified in continuing to attend rituals. The other reason was the not unnatural one that I had no ancestors, and although I was soon given quasi-kinship status, as I have said, it was perhaps going a little too far to include me as a practicing and sacrificing kinsman. However, the time came when I was able to witness a few sacrifices, and then to participate in them as a member or quasi-member of the lineage concerned. When it clearly did not affect the outcome of the rite, my presence was accepted; and I think that my polite and obviously sincere and unpatronizing curiosity about their religious beliefs and acts was appreciated.

My notes of the time show that I was told of a large variety of rituals, none of which seemed to have any common pattern except that some of the Lugbara terms were the same throughout. I was later to realize that these words were important, as in the understanding of their precise meaning lay the way to understanding Lugbara religion itself. From my interviews I began to see that Lugbara made offerings to the ghosts of their ancestors and to various aspects of Divinity or of spirits. The offerings were usually made as a consequence of sickness, thought to be sent to a sinner or offender against proper moral behavior. If he recovered, an offering would be made to the mystical power that had been shown to be responsible at consultation with oracles or diviners. The offerings consisted of various animals or of grain. I was also told that two important elements of the rite were that the ghosts would send sickness as a consequence of their invocation by the living, and that after the sacrifice the living members of the group concerned would eat of the sacrificial meat. I tried day after day when reading through my notes in the evening to discern some kind of pattern in the ways in which the various elements of this process were organized, but found it impossible. It seemed clear enough, therefore, that this was not the way to go about studying Lugbara sacrifice. Religious beliefs and actions cannot be studied in isolation from one another and the remainder of the culture as though they were disconnected elements; they are elements set together within a single system of thought and belief. My immediate problem therefore was to understand what was their organization or pattern; and since as religious beliefs they were symbols, I had to discover what was the reality that they symbolized. It was clear that an understanding of the unity underlying them could be gained only by observation of and participation in the ritual acts that were also elements in the same system.

At last I was invited to attend a sacrifice. For this I had to wait for several months. Doubtless I could have pushed my way into a sacrificial gathering without waiting to be invited, but I could see no good reason for doing so. For one thing I had a great many other matters to study; for another my knowledge of the language was not adequate to understand what was being said when several people were talking rapidly together—as they seemed to be doing most of the time; and lastly it seemed to me that rudeness on my part in this regard would have been badly construed by my hosts (indeed, it would have been worse than rudeness). I was aware that while I was observing the Lugbara they were continually observing me. At first they were interested in my material possessions and my ordinary everyday behavior. But their interest in these matters was soon satisfied and they became concerned with more important things. The Lugbara, like members of any other small-scale society, lived their lives in close personal contact with one another and within a closely knit network of kin and neighborhood relations. This meant that they were extremely conscious of small nuances of behavior and motivation and this was what they were interested in with regard to myself. It was clear that any too great interest on my part in other than the most mundane events would be taken as a sign of ill-intent and hostility toward them. I therefore bided my time, hoping that sooner or later it would become a natural thing for me to attend sacrifices. It was certainly frustrating day after day to hear gossip about various rituals being performed in the neighborhood, but I waited patiently and I think that I was right to do so. I was later to find out that many members of the local neighborhood were very ready to think that I was a witch or sorcerer; one of the signs of such a person is that he will attempt to scrounge food while passing other people's homesteads, or, worst of all, will try to harm people directly by intruding into sacrifices in which people are in close and intimate relationship with their ancestors.

The chance came quite casually one morning when I was walking past a compound filled with people drinking and talking—the hubbub was extraordinarily loud and could be heard half a mile away—and was invited in by some of the men there whom I knew. This was a small sacrifice to the ghosts on behalf of a young man who had been sick for some time and who had recently recovered. Nobody took much notice of me, as by this time I was well known as a drinking companion to many of them. The sacrifice was just beginning, and I was invited to sit down and watch what was going on. Two goats had already been slaughtered and were now being skinned. Women were cooking millet and vegetables and were serving beer. After some time the Elder of the group stood up and talked quietly for some five minutes in very rapid words. I could not understand much of what he said but he was clearly discussing the nature of the sickness and of the events that led up to it. Some of the meat was brought to him with a small bowl of fresh blood from the animals. He sat down near the shrines and placed some of the meat on them and poured some of the blood over them. He then stood up, took some leaves in his left hand, and walked up and down talking in a loud voice. After he had spoken, one or two of the other older men did also. There seemed to be a good deal of argument between them and I was told that this was because their words had to be "true" words. Finally they went to the young man who had been sick and was sitting near his hut, spat on his face and blew into his ears. The Elder then took more of the blood and smeared it on the chest and ankles of the youth, and then poured a little on the thresholds of the huts and on the earth by the compound gateway. Some women then brought some of the cooked meat and the assembled men moved into small groups to eat it and to drink beer. The Elder ate quickly and then took some of the uncooked meat and divided it into small piles on the ground. When the men had finished eating and drinking, which took perhaps an hour and a half, they took some of the small piles of meat and staggered off homeward singing drunkenly as they went.

I also returned home to sit sadly and to think that if this was all there was to a sacrifice I could not see why it was so important to the Lugbara and what all the fuss was about. I have set this down very briefly in order to show the kind of sketchy impressions that one is liable to get from first observations of rites of this kind. Later on when I knew more about the nature of Lugbara sacrifices I was able to take coherent and meaningful notes on what I saw, but this took several months. In any kind of event in any culture it is difficult, if not impossible, to obtain a coherent and significant idea of what one sees if one does not know exactly what one is looking for. This may sound very obvious and indeed it is, but I think it is important for an understanding of anthropological fieldwork. Many months later I was able to go to a sacrifice of this kind and to understand most if not all of the shades of behavior that I witnessed. These were obviously many, since a rite of this kind encapsulates within it many social relationships, tensions, conflicts, and ambitions, and is a dramatic enactment of complex change in a network of ties between kin of various kinds. But at first I was not aware of this because I was too ignorant of the overall organization of the local community, and also because I regarded a sacrifice as a single performance or event. It is that, of course, but it is very much more.

During the next month, having once broken the ice and once my neighbors had realized that my presence had not harmed the efficacy of that rite, I attended many more sacrifices. Some of these were slight with only a handful of people present, while others would be attended by fifty or sixty men and last all day. The object of sacrifice varied very considerably, as did both the forms of behavior and even the order in which the various events took place. I began to realize that there were two basic problems for investigation here. One was the organization and aims of the rite itself, and the other was in the train of events that led up to it. It is most convenient to describe how I investigated these matters one by one, although this is of course a distortion of how I actually did this.

The first problem, that of the structure of the ritual, is one that I need not go into at any great length. At first I thought that the immense variation in detail was due to individual whim, and to some extent this was true. But I realized that there was a consistent structure to all these rites and that they could be divided into three main sections. These were marked in each case by the giving of a ritual address by the man in charge of the sacrifice. The first phase, the end of which was marked by the first address, was concerned with calling living and dead members of the group together and with the mechanics of slaughter and preparation of the offering. The second was that in which the ghosts and spirits would consume the offering; that phase was ended by the second ritual address. The third phase was marked by the sharing of the sacrificial meat by the living members of the congregation. This was, of course, a classic example of a *rite de passage* as described by Van Gennep and by Hubert and Mauss. Most of the variations from one rite to another, I soon came to realize, were due largely to details of the second set of problems mentioned above (that of the antecedent train of events); I had therefore to turn to these and put the individual rites into a wider social context in order to understand the rites themselves.

Oracles and Diviners

To gain this understanding I had to turn to getting information about notions of sickness, sin, the relationship between these, sacrifice, and the dead. Here obviously I had to devote most attention to acquiring data from informants; they could hardly be observed as I would observe a sacrifice. The Lugbara believed that most sickness came as a consequence of sin, and was usually sent by the dead. It was said that the dead hear the words of the living and then send sickness to show the offender, whose offence is that of disobedience to his elders, the error of his ways. It was clear, to me at any rate, that this process did not in fact happen in any sense of scientific reality. But what did happen was the next stage in the process. This was the consultation of oracles and diviners. They were used to provide the answer to how the sickness had occurred, and according to oracular statements the details of the later sacrificial ritual were arranged. I therefore had to use two kinds of informants here. One comprised the older men who were thought to invoke the dead, and the other comprised the oracle operators themselves.

I found this easy to do, since part of its significance is that an oracle was consulted openly and in public. It was therefore simple enough to spend many hours sitting with one or two old men and the operator, observing what went on. The greatest difficulty was always that I knew too little about the lineage history of the people concerned in any particular case. But at least I realized how important it was. I had the great fortune fairly early to make the acquaintance of a renowned oracle operator, a man called Ayua (whose photograph is on the cover of *The Lugbara of Uganda*). We took a liking to each other, and I think that he found my interest in his work both flattering and profitable, not in the sense that I paid him but that it increase his local reputation to have what the Lugbara saw as an apprentice. I started by learning the nature of the various oracles used and then learned how to make them myself. At least therefore I was able to learn the rudiments of their operation, although I never operated them as a professional. I spent many days sitting with Ayua while he talked with me about oracles and the powers that he thought lie behind them, and about the whole process of the invocation of the dead and the sacrifices made to them. Also of course I saw a great many consultations, since men would come to his homestead to consult him. I was therefore able to do several things. One was to learn a good deal of the operation of oracles and of their place in Lugbara social life, and also something of the whole process of sacrifice; but I was also able to understand the importance of the local community and of the relationships within it as a single system in which there was always change, development, and conflict. I realized the significance of sacrifice only at this point. Any one rite is but one in long-lasting—perhaps everlasting—series of rites, of which a main purpose is to accommodate change and conflict within a small lineage and neighborhood. The variations in detail that I have mentioned and that I found so confusing when I witnessed them were due to this very fact. Rituals, as has often been said, are ways of stating relations of power and authority; they are ways of expressing a man's position and aspirations in a total system of social relations. The more important sacrifices were occasions for the restructuring of lineage genealogies and thereby of relations of authority within the lineage and neighborhood. I finally realized that perhaps the best way of understanding this process would be to take a single lineage group and to analyze its history in detail and the series of rituals performed by its various members. This sounds a little more deliberate than was perhaps the case, but I found that I knew much more about one small lineage (that I have called Araka) than any

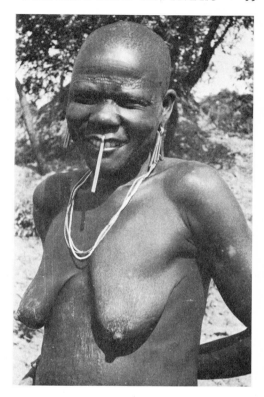

An old woman of A'dumi. She wears lip- and ear-pins made locally of iron. She had borne seven children of whom four were living, had nine grandchildren and two great-grandchildren. She married at about the age of twelve and was about fifty years old when the photograph was taken.

other, and devoted a good deal of time to the careful study of its growth and development. I have described this in detail in Chapter 4 of my book *Lugbara Religion*. But there is one point that may merit mention. This is that I was not here using the well-worn and long-tried method of illustrating an explanation of social events and relationships by describing case histories: that has had a long history in anthropological field research and is obviously valuable. What I did was to take a single social group and study it over as long a time as was possible, so that my explanation was made in terms of a series of case histories all of which were related causally to one another over time. I think that this was far more valuable than merely quoting a string of unconnected cases, which is essentially the Frazerian approach and lacks a sense of sociological interdependence between events and persons.

I found that my work with Ayua was of the utmost value, especially since by this time I already possessed a fairly wide knowledge of the society so that I could place his role within it fairly accurately. I think that to have depended upon a single informant in this way during the first year of my fieldwork would have been misleading. I had had, however, one such informant after the first few months of work. This was an elderly lady who was a diviner and doctor. She, like all her kind, was a somewhat eccentric and uncanny person and much feared in the neighborhood. She divined in the darkness of her hut, and could cure various mystically caused sicknesses by sucking out objects from the victims' bodies. She was also a midwife who was called in difficult circumstances. I had myself been called in in one such situation, as I relate below, and I learned afterward that she had heard of this and had wondered who I was. However, the incident that caused us to begin a fairly close relationship was a pure accident. As I have said, I spent an hour or so each day treating small wounds and sicknesses, and one day when walking past her homestead I was called in to see her. She had spilt boiling water over her legs and was in great pain, with serious burns. I was able to ease her pain with simple medicines and helped her recover perhaps more quickly than she would otherwise have done. In return she taught me about local drugs and ways of treating sickness, as well as basic notions as to the etiology of disease. I spent many hours with her, both writing down notes on her work and occasionally watching her in action as a diviner. Although this was useful to me I think that it was in many ways a mistake, since unlike oracle operators the work of diviners is secret and my presence there, I discovered later, was resented by those consulting her. If I could have met her later it would have been better.

My work with this lady did have one useful consequence, which was that interest was taken in my work by a local Christian evangelist who was also a school teacher and herbalist. I already knew this man fairly well but our relationship had not been easy, because in his role as Christian pastor he could not openly approve of my interest in traditional Lugbara culture. But when he realized that I had an interest in medicine, of which he had great knowledge, this immediately gave us something in common. One morning therefore he came to visit me holding his Bible, which was both for him and for his patients an integral part of his power. He maintained that his work was that of God and that it was right that I should know of it both as an antidote to my learning of the "words of Satan" (as the missionaries called the cult of the dead), and because he thought that his knowledge of good traditional medicines should be spread to a wider world. We spent many days together traveling through the woodland collecting specimens of plants, roots, and leaves. I also watched him curing many sick people, in particular those afflicted by sorcery who suffered from various kinds of trance and fit. His real importance to me, however, was that he was able to introduce me to the field of Christian evangelists and prophetic leaders.

Religion and Change

During the time I was in Lugbaraland there were a good many Christian Lugbara scattered across the country. Missions had been working in the area since before 1920, being represented by the English missionaries of the Africa Inland Mission and by the Italians of the Verona Fathers. I have already mentioned something of my relationship with the missionaries themselves. But I had a closer relationship with ordinary Lugbara Christians; some of these were orthodox adherents of the missions and others were adherents of various breakaway movements that had originated in Christian mission activities and had become somewhat unorthodox in their beliefs. These latter people were scattered throughout Lugbaraland under the leadership of evangelists and prophets. They had broken away from the authority of the missions and from mission-taught Christianity. Most of the ordinary members were women and still under the authority of fathers and husbands, while the leaders themselves were eccentric and bizarre men who were, not unnaturally, extremely suspicious of Europeans, whom they equated with orthodox Christians. Although I did not do as much work among these people as I now wish I had done, they were clearly of considerable significance for an understanding of Lugbara society and its history. I made contact with some of these prophetic leaders simply by calling on them toward the end of my stay. By that time I knew enough about Lugbara society and of the role of these men in it as to know what I was doing. I was able to discuss their tenets with them and was permitted to attend some of their meetings.

What is significant here is the problem that all fieldworkers must face when studying the religious beliefs of another people. The Lugbara knew, when I asked them questions about their beliefs in their traditional religion and when I took part in sacrifices to the dead and to spirits, that I did not hold these beliefs to be true in the way that they did. I never found the least difficulty in this position and was never asked by pagan Lugbara whether or not I believed in the existence of the dead and in their powers in the way that they did. Often they would ask me about by own religious beliefs and I would explain that whatever my own beliefs I did not regard them as being the only true ones possible. It was generally assumed that I was a Christian, since Christianity was the faith held, rather intolerantly, by people who had power whatever their ethnic origins, unless they happened to be Muslims. But the situation was very different when I talked with those Lugbara who regarded themselves as being Christians, whether they were orthodox adherents or not. As I have said, they were suspicious of me because they assumed I was spying on them on behalf of the missionaries. On the other hand they were very proud of the beliefs they held and considered themselves to be chosen people. There was therefore a certain amount of hostility in our initial conversations. This soon lapsed, since it was obvious that I was not ridiculing them nor reporting on what they were doing to the government or to the missions. I was perhaps helped inadvertently by a rumor that some of the missionaries were angry to hear that I drank beer and went to dances. Also possibly the mere fact that a European, even such an odd one as I appeared to be, was interested in them and talked to them on equal terms may have given them some grounds to trust me.

I did, however, miss one aspect of the role of these religious leaders that I was to realize only after my final return from Uganda. This was their role as the instigators and agents of radical social change. I think now that I was not impressed by them at the time in that they appeared to be marginal to everyday social life: most Lugbara may have met some of these people but took little note of them, partly because they lacked political power. Yet I can see clearly enough today that they were among the harbingers of social change and were indeed in the tradition of the great prophet Rembe who led the Lugbara at various times during the early years of Western impact.

When I worked in northern Lugbara I soon became aware of the importance of Rembe. He was an historical personage, who spent some time in Lugbara at the time of the First World War. He organized a new form of

Lugbara society and was deported and hanged in the Sudan in 1917. I heard his name mentioned on several occasions, until one day I asked about him deliberately. I had already read something about his movement in the still-extant government files of the period that were stored in an ant-infested shed at Arua, and so knew the official version of his activities. My first inquiries were met with obvious embarrassment, and I was passed from one man to another, each older and more respected. Finally I was formally invited to attend a meeting of senior men so that they could tell me "the words of Rembe" which I was to write down in my notebook. I found that the leader was a friend of mine, Khalfan Simandre, a man of late middle-age and a sub-county chief whose father had been one of Rembe's close associates. His role was that of the son of his famous father and also official government representative who could assure the others that in telling me of what had been an antigovernment movement that had culminated in a revolt in 1919, they would be quite secure from any possible disapproval. To my astonishment the five old gentlemen who interviewed me spoke more and more freely and excitedly about what I suddenly realized was possibly the single most important historical event for them within living memory. We met all day for three days and our discussion covered all that they could remember of the years from 1890 until 1920, the period of first European impact.

Rembe was regarded by them as a mythological figure, and they spoke about him in the same mythopoeic idiom as they would describe the two hero-ancestors, Dribidu and Jaki. They did not tell of his activities in the terms they would use to describe an ordinary person, despite the fact that they had all known Rembe as closely as anyone could have. For example, they described in detail the immediate source of his power, a many-colored snake or lizard with a man's face, that dwelt in a pool in Oleiba that I was taken to see; I was told that Rembe climbed to the tops of trees and there walked across the top of the patches of forest in the area; and many other wonders. I knew that when these events took place in 1916 the participants had often been under the influence of drugs, but they were certainly not so when they spoke about them with me in 1951. It was impossible for me to discover how they themselves really intended these statements to be understood, but they certainly believed in what they told me. They were using a mythopoeic form of speech so as to indicate Rembe's divine qualities. At first I found it difficult to accept such language when used of actual persons whose actual behavior had been witnessed by my informants. But once I realized that they would relate to me certain events that had taken place thirty-five years before, referring to all the personages except Rembe in terms of "ordinary" people, and reserving the mythopoeic idiom for Rembe's behavior only, then I grasped that they were showing that he was an emissary of Divine Spirit and therefore not an ordinary man at all. They saw him as a Divine agent coming to lead them back to a happier Paradise that they had lost because of the impact of the outside world.

Another point is that they never related these important events to me in any kind of chronogical order. Rembe had featured in their lives on two occasions: first when some of them had visited him in Kakwa country (he was a Kakwa, not a Lugbara) about 1895, and when he visited them some time between 1914 and 1917. Between those dates they had witnessed the establishment of Belgian,

Sudanese, and British rule in turn, and had experienced immense changes in their everyday lives. But when telling me about Rembe, his contacts with them were usually put together and only by implication given any connection with the other events I have mentioned—which in fact were those to which his behavior was a response. I have mentioned the same kind of ahistoricity when describing the Lugbara myths of origin; it was part of a mythopoeic idiom quite unlike our own Western sense of "historical" time.

The point I am making here is one that I have mentioned briefly before. It is that one cannot reconstruct past events unless one already knows the basic historiographical and mythopoeic idioms of the people who are relating their "history." I was, after all, interested in the early history of colonial impact on the Lugbara, and wanted to know how they had responded to it. I was told a mass of "facts," as the Lugbara saw them, but always through a mythopoeic prism: although by "common sense" the "facts" hardly made sense (although doubtless I could have forced them into some kind of mold easily enough), being neither apparently truthful nor put into any kind of chronogical order, once I grasped the idiom used they fell into meaningful place at once.

The Patterning of Information

I have used the example of my trying to understand the principles of Lugbara religious belief and practice in order to point out some of the relevant methodological problems. I am not holding up the particular way that I did this as a model for others: much depends on the nature of the society and its members, who, as I have said at the beginning of this book, showed me their way of life in their own way with the emphases that seemed important to them. But clearly if there were no basic principles of anthropological research there would be no point in my writing this book. It seems to me, looking back at what I tried to do when learning about Lugbara religion, that there are two main methodological points to be made. One is the way in which I conceived the anthropological study of religion, as such; the other is the method I used to discover the significance of data, as distinct from the data themselves. Fieldwork is a means by which one selects some data (a small proportion of the data available to observation) and discards others. This is not the place to discuss these problems at length but they are worthy of brief mention.

I found very soon that there was little point in adding more and more facts to my notes. Clearly at first I had to collect any material that came to me: my ignorance of Lugbara culture was such that I had to build up a basic set of data in order to obtain any knowledge of the principal elements of their culture and social organization. But, as I have shown, my first months' fieldwork yielded little except for an increasing knowledge of the language—it was essentially a period that I had to get through before I could start on the real part of the work.

It is not easy to describe very clearly any exact process of building up a body of data which made sense to me as a means of understanding what I saw day after day. I spent a good deal of time writing rough drafts of reports on my work, although they were merely convenient ways of putting my mind in order and were not intended for publication or perusal by others. I have always found that my own way of working requires a good deal of putting on paper—others may not work in the same way. But by trying to write down summaries and conclusions, by building up patterns and structures on paper, I was able to consider various hypotheses that I could then test by asking specific questions about them. I could thus fill in gaps and also realize whether or not I was on the right track.

Let me give an example. I have referred to it already when I mentioned the many variations in detail of sacrifices. The Lugbara made sacrificial offerings of cattle, goats, sheep, chickens, and grain; they offered them to ghosts, ancestors (each of several categories—patrilineal, matrilateral, and so on), and to several categories of spirits; they made these sacrifices in response to various kinds of sickness, associated with various kinds of sins and offenses. There were thus four sets of variables (oblation; spiritual agent; sickness; and offense) for which I assumed that there would be a neat pattern of relationships. I spent many months seeking this pattern, but it eluded me. I then thought, as I mentioned earlier, that the key factor might have been individual whim only—in other words, there would be no consistent pattern. Finally I saw that the key factor in the pattern was the historical development of the sacrificing group, so that I had to turn to the study of the cycle of development of lineages and sections in order to understand the pattern in the organization of sacrificial rites.

The point I am making is simple but I think important. No fieldworker can collect every item of cultural behavior—or at least it seems to me to be highly unlikely—although he can certainly obtain an astonishing amount of data in his year or two in the field. It is a question of knowing what is relevant. The only way of knowing that, it seems to me, is to appreciate the patterns built up of cultural elements, and the only way of doing this is periodically to work out a number of possible hypotheses that at least make a pattern of some kind of completeness or incompleteness from what data one has already. One difficulty is that this work can only be done to any real extent away from the everyday distractions of the field, and this for most of us means after our fieldwork has ended and we are writing dissertations, papers, or books. But we can at least start this process in the field.

6

Conclusion: The End of Fieldwork

I HAVE DISCUSSED certain aspects of what I did during the two-year period that I spent among the Lugbara. I have not kept the account in any chronological order, for the reason that I mentioned at the beginning of this book. In this final chapter I wish to put what I have written so far into a more general framework.

The Study of Cultural Variation

During the time I was there I worked in four parts of Lugbaraland, as well as visiting other areas of the country. I have already described the first area, in south-central Lugbaraland. After about nine months there I decided that I should work elsewhere and moved to northern Lugbaraland for a few weeks, then to western Lugbara on the Congo border, then briefly to the eastern part of the country, and then back to the same part of northern Lugbara that I had already visited. I spent most of the second year there, with a couple of weeks in southern Uganda, in Lugbara settlement of cotton farmers in Buganda and Bunyoro.

The three other areas in Lugbaraland itself were basically very similar to that in which I had already spent many months. But, partly because I had taken care to spend those months in one area, so that I knew it very well (as well, I suppose, as I know any place on earth), the differences in detail were immediately obvious to me. The area of western Lugbara, on the Congo border, was A'dumi. I was very unhappy there. The main reason was that I was again in the position of a newly arrived stranger, without friends or "kin"; but in addition this was an area of much intermingling of small groups of different clan affiliations, which had taken refuge there after having moved from the harsher colonial regime over the border in the Congo. There was considerable competition for land and power, and it was an area notorious for its sorcery. For a time I thought that my discovery of the importance of sorcery and of the persistent malice and hostility that lay behind it were due to my own sense of frustration and longing for the relatively ordered

61

life I had left behind me in my earlier place of work. But at least I was soon aware of this possibility and realized that it did not explain what I found, although it certainly was the cause for my sour remarks about the people there in my diary of the period.

After a short stay of four weeks, I spent some weeks among the eastern Lugbara of Omugo. This was an area much affected by Islam and the scene of some of the early hostility to the colonial administration that culminated in the Rembe-inspired revolt of 1919 at Udupi, to which I have already referred. Here my dissatisfaction that had been so obvious during my stay at A'dumi died down, as I was able again to see the importance of the marked differences in cultural detail from the area I knew so well from my first year. Unfortunately I found that I could understand very little of the local dialect, so that my progress was very slow and the results as far as filling pages of notes very disappointing. The differences from the first area were also marked enough for me to realize that I could not build on what I had learnt there. But whereas A'dumi had struck me as an area of some disintegration from what I asssumed to be a more "traditional" system, it was very clear that Omugo, Udupi, Aringa, and the other parts of eastern and northeastern Lugbaraland could in no way be regarded in that light. They were simply very different from what I had experienced during the previous year. This made me reconsider my view of A'dumi, and I returned there for a week to see whether I had merely been misled in what I had learnt there. That week, although short, enabled me to view A'dumi more dispassionately and to put my experience there in proper perspective. These weeks also taught me something that I was not fully to appreciate until much later, when I spent a short time in Metu, among the western Madi: that the cultural variations within Lugbara were as great as between them and the Madi, their related neighbors to the east.

I spent the remainder of my fieldwork period in one place in north-central Lugbara, called Maraca (in which was the lineage "Araka" that I have mentioned above). I chose this for several reasons. It was the center of a densely populated region, near the heartland of the country close to Mounts Eti and Liru; it was said to be very "traditional" in many ways, yet had been the scene of the first colonial administrative center established by the Belgians in 1900. Also I had very friendly relations with the county chief who lived a few miles from where I did, at a place he called Ovujo, "the house of idleness"; with the local sub-county chief, he who introduced me to the men who told me about the prophet Rembe; and with my cook's father, who lived a little way from where I established myself. I had stayed there for short periods during the previous year. I knew, therefore, that here I had kin ready-made, as it were, and was able to gain a great amount of valuable data which provided me with the bulk of the worthwhile information I collected during the total research period. Much of the work described in previous chapters was done in Maraca, although I have not explicitly mentioned the changes in locale in them. I was able to come to this area with both a considerable knowledge of Lugbara culture in general, with a knowledge of what I was looking for, and with a fresh eye. I saw everything as though for the first time, but with some knowledge of its likely significance and its relevance to my own work. Here I also took on another helper, Oraa, a local man of some age but a younger full-brother of an Elder: he was therefore near the sources of local power and knowledge but was not himself concerned to exercise it. He was ideal as introducer and also as informant.

There is no need to relate what I did in Maraca in detail; it was a continuation of what I had done already and the methodological points have already been mentioned. But there is one point that should be made. By this time I was aware of the general pattern of Lugbara culture and social organization, so that I no longer regarded items of behavior as isolated but could expect, and grasp when I saw them, the relations between them. In other words, I was able by this time to comprehend the totality of everyday social behavior much as did the Lugbara themselves. If I observed farming, for example, I was aware of the general cosmological background to it; if I heard a discussion about witchcraft I could place it within the wider system of notions of sin, sacrifice, lineage segmentation, conflict for authority, and so on. In brief, I was aware not only of the interrelationships between one item of behavior and another but also of the bounds of Lugbara culture. Before this I had always been aware that there could be a vast range of behavior of which I knew nothing; by now, although of course I continued to collect new details of culture until the last day of my stay, I knew what was the totality of cultural detail and variation that I was likely to find. This was not, however, a time when all I had left to do was to fill in a few gaps of detail; I had rather to continue to seek out those relations between items of behavior and belief that I had not realized existed, and—perhaps more important since after all everything is ultimately related in one way or another to everything else—to weigh the significance of each relationship in the totality of Lugbara culture.

Interviews and Other Mundane Matters

Although I do not wish to discuss field "techniques" as such, I should say something about how I carried out interviews with informants. I have read in accounts of fieldwork methodology about the various ways of structuring interviews, with the implication that this is necessary for any successful gathering of data. I do not believe that this is true. It is clear from my own experience among the Lugbara that I found myself in four kinds of interview situations. The first was that in which I would be sitting among a mass of people who were engaged in drinking beer or performing a ceremony or ritual where my presence was to them merely peripheral and of little importance. On these occasions I would participate as far as I could in whatever was going on, which usually meant drinking, eating, and making as much sense as I could out of the hubbub of conversation around me. I suppose this merits the term "interview-situation." I know that on many occasions I very much wanted to interrupt what was going on with questions, but I never did. The main point of my being there was to observe the whole process and flow of activity in a given situation and I tried to be as inconspicuous as I could and to observe as much as I could for later questioning. If you like, these were preparatory interviews in which I would mark in my notebook and in my own mind points that I could discuss more privately later. They were also important in that my mere presence as an observer and participant was witness to my role of merely being an observer. On these occasions I showed myself to be above board, to be interested in the everyday life around me, and as far as I was able to behave as an ordinary person. It was rare on these occasions that there was not some stranger present whom I would notice asking puzzled but discreet questions about me. He would be told that I was the man who was learning Lugbara culture and history so that I could tell people in Europe about it. The questioner would accept this information with a nod (as my reputation spread quickly) and often with a smile and a handshake for me. I have given an example of this kind of interview, if it may be called that, in discussing my first presence at ritual performances. From the point of view of filling out my notes these occasions yielded little, but from that of understanding the life around me they were invaluable.

The second type of interview situation was that in which I would sit with two or three people, perhaps a man, his wife, and children, or a couple of men working in a field, and would discuss matters of interest with some care and with myself asking fairly carefully thought out questions. By that I do not mean that I thought out the phrases that I would use, but that I would try to ask my questions in a particular sequence in order to fill in points on which I wanted particular information. On many occasions these discussions became inconsequential as the people themselves would grow interested and excited, either because I was talking about something that was important to be told to me or important to be hidden from me. I would always try not to guide the conversation too much since I found after the first few months that if I did so either the people would grow bored or it would not occur to them to fill in the gaps in my own knowledge that would have been of interest to me had I known about them. These interviews were important for two reasons: from them I could fill in gaps of information and could ask for more detailed accounts than would be possible to obtain in general discussions with large numbers of people present; and because again they enabled me to make friends and to see the main lines of Lugbara culture open out before me. At these times I always wrote in a notebook and would transcribe my notes the same evening if I could possibly do so, with the date and identity of the informants. I could also take photographs much more easily at these times than when in a large mass of people, when there was always likely to be someone who did not like the idea.

The third type of interview was probably the most profitable as far as filling up my notebooks was concerned. These were long discussions with one person. I found that at any one time I would have one or two cronies who would play for a period of a week or two the role of inseparable confidant. Their motives were many and mixed. At times they were people who would gain prestige by being with me. Sometimes they would get a great deal of beer from me; sometimes they thought they could pay off old grudges by gossiping about their enemies. I think that this kind of interview situation is universal in anthropological field-work, and although it is very valuable it is not always easy to deal with. The Lugbara, although they lack marked differences of wealth or status, are extremely competitive and jealous people. So that bosom friendships of this kind can be somewhat harmful unless very carefully handled. At the same time the Lugbara are friendly people and I was not willing to snub a man who was merely trying to be helpful because of the risk of being involved in personal quarrels. My childhood had been spent largely near a small town near London, but with regular and extended holidays among farm people of a small and remote hamlet. In that village I, as a kinsman of a locally important farmer, had been in a situation not unlike that in which I found myself among the Lugbara. I was a stranger, and though a fairly wealthy one was yet a young man who did not show obvious signs of snobbishness and wished to be friendly with everybody. In other words I am saying that I tended in Lugbaraland to play by ear and to let things come as they might. Looking back I think now that I should perhaps have taken greater care not to have let myself be involved in various obscure interpersonal quarrels and jealousies. On the other hand the mere fact that I was told about these quarrels and jealousies was extremely valuable and indeed essential, especially when I began to analyze the cycle of lineage segmentation and the concomitant rites of sacrifice. All that I can really say here is that I behaved in exactly the same way as would anyone involved in the everyday life of any small village or neighborhood. I respected confidences and tried not to give offense, and tried to preserve an Olympian detachment from local quarrels and a sense of understanding and compassion. I come here to what is probably the single most difficult problem that faces an anthropologist: living among people who are themselves living out their everyday lives as does everyone in any society anywhere, but at the same time trying hard to remain outside these local relationships and to be an impartial observer of them. I admit that living with people such as the Lugbara, whose culture is in many ways so different from my own, many events that caused them to feel anger, guilt, or shame, were not events that caused me to feel the same sentiments nor even to imagine myself feeling them in those situations. There were also many situations when by observation or from gossip I learned of various actions that I found objectionable, but I would later have to talk with their perpetrators as though I cared nothing about their doings and when I knew that by doing precisely nothing would cause those people who had told me about the actions to feel that I was two-faced or cowardly in not regarding the people concerned in the way that they did themselves. These are matters on which one can advise a would-be fieldworker only by suggesting to him that he observe common sense and good manners and maintain a sense of decency and of understanding the weaknesses of other people. If this sounds smug and pretentious then I can answer only that I know no other advice.

The last type of interview situation was the somewhat different one of interviewing a person while filling in a questionnaire. I used questionnaires on several occasions. The first comprised four surveys that I made in different parts of the country to obtain some basic demographic information, with emphasis on the patterns of marriage within the group and with its neighbors. In each case I took a major section as the relevant group (some five to eight hundred people), and obtained data from every household in the section's territory. I had the questionnaire duplicated, in Lugbara, a single form covering all the members of a single homestead. I found that it would take me almost a morning to complete one form, so that I obviously had to have help. I asked the local mission-run secondary schools for assistance, and found a few schoolboys from each of the actual groups I wished to survey who were willing to help me in their school vacations. These were the only people who I actually paid in cash, by the day, for helping me. After spending a few days showing them what was required, we would visit every compound covered by the survey to introduce ourselves, and my assistants returned later to fill in the forms. They were of much value to me, and I wish that I had been able to do more of this work. I should add here that this was done toward the end of my stay, when I knew exactly what I wanted and when I could use questionnaires not to elicit fresh cultural details but rather to provide quantitative demonstration of processes of which I already knew the outlines. The work took a couple of months in each area.

As I have said, this was a slow process and I left most of the donkeywork to my helpers. However, from the few questionnaires that I did myself I found that if I spent an hour in filling in the replies to the actual questions on the paper I would spend at least another hour and a half in discussing them. I found that it was usually impossible to answer the questions in the order set out on the paper but that I had instead to fill them in in the order in which they occurred spontaneously in the course of conversation. I found also, and this is perhaps important, that information gained by questionnaire could be of a very superficial and public nature and I always took great care to administer them in public with as many people standing around listening, giving advice, and volunteering information of their own, as cared to attend. On one occasion I remember clearly administering half a dozen questionnaires to half a dozen people at the same time, trying to go down the list of questions going from one informant to another before passing on to the next question. The noise of argument must have carried a good quarter of a mile, but at least it was obvious that I was not hiding anything; despite the grievous departure from strict canons of technique in administering a questionnaire, such a way of doing it was certainly better in the Lugbara situation than sitting carefully and cold-bloodedly with a single person at a time. One must remember that as far as Lugbara of that time were concerned, virtually no one in the audience could read the marks I wrote on the pieces of paper, so that the more publicity given to what I was doing the better it was.

In passing I must admit that I can still only wonder at the kindness and patience of the many people with whom I spoke, often about matters of considerable intimacy, and that the degree of trust shown in me was really astonishing. I think that it is important and indeed wish to stress the fact that all depends upon one's own approach to one's informants. I have heard of anthropologists who have had chiefs and others in power punish people who refused to give information, and I have heard of others who will pay people or even get them drunk to get them to divulge secret information on matters that they would normally prefer not to discuss with strangers. I have also known anthropologists who have acquired confidential information and then use it in later interviews to illicit still further confidential information from other informants. It seems to me that such behavior is intolerable. I am not saying that I made no mistakes with informants but at least I did not break confidences or publish confidential information. The Lugbara accepted me as a guest and a friend and I tried to behave properly in these roles.

The Role of Fieldworker

By the end of two years in the field I had acquired a status in Lugbara eyes that appeared to be a reasonably stable one. I have mentioned early in this book something of the rather ill-defined roles that I had been given at the beginning of my stay. I had essentially been given, first, the status of a human being; then the incipient or uncertain semi-status of an immature social being, a stranger; then a more clearly definable and acceptable full status of a social or socialized being. I had, as I have mentioned, begun the development into a fully mature social being that is gone through, much more gradually and carefully, by a growing child and by a stranger who enters a Lugbara community from outside.

In the beginning the role I played was associated—with one exception—with technical activities: I was concerned with farming, hut-building, making spears and drums, and the like. The symbolic content of what I did and learned was minimal, and whatever such content there was was at the time almost beyond my comprehension. The exception, of course, was that at first I was given the role of European and so a man of power and nontraditional authority: this role became increasingly anomalous as I was given a more socialized total status in Lugbara society, and eventually the contradiction had to be resolved.

The change in role in the first year was expressed mainly in being allotted a status defined in terms of quasi-kinship. I hope that I have explained the nature of this enough to make it meaningful. Its acquisition was preceded by the various events that marked a change in my status from "thing" to "person": eating, drinking, dancing, and so on, and with events that marked the gradual loss of my "European" status, such as the invitation to drink *waragi* at the site of an illicit still.

The status of European, insofar as it was possible for it to be dropped—after all, it was not possible for me to drop it completely, since I *was* a European and not a Lugbara in any final analysis—was removed from me after about eight months. I was not all that aware of this process at the time it took place, but I saw later what it represented. The first development was not a single event but a series of occasions at which I took part in various activities at which European administrators and missionaries as well as Lugbara—both "New People" and ordinary persons—participated. They included various government holidays, with parades at the district headquarters in Arua; religious festivals and school celebrations, held at the two missions, and odd meetings and conversations with European officials. I noticed more and more that on these occasions, some formal, others not, I was increasingly placed on the Lugbara side. Whatever the situation, it was not unexpectedly always regarded by the Lugbara as one for the expression of the then basic axis of conflict in the region—Lugbara versus the others, or less commonly, Africans versus the others. I was counted more and more as being on the Lugbara side, perhaps as a Fifth Column agent of the Lugbara pretending to be on the other side but in reality "our child," "the child of Nyio" and similar phrases. I need not enlarge on this point, and perhaps I am exaggerating the significance of these incidents, but I noticed that when later discussing them I was increasingly included among the "we" rather than among "those Europeans."

Another occasion was to me both important and frightening. I was called about midnight to go to the hut of a young married woman, whose family I by then knew quite well, who was in childbirth. It was a breech birth and she was very weak from pneumonia. After many hours' labor, her mother, an old lady with whom I had often joked using the obscenities of a Lugbara joking relationship (since by some roundabout way I was reckoned as her husband's sister's son), suggested that I be called in. By this time it was known that my closest friend among the local Europeans was the doctor, so that it was assumed that I had unlimited medical expertise. When I reached the hut the woman was very weak. Obviously I was medically unskilled and other than suggesting that fewer old women and less herbal smoke in the hut might help, there was not much that I could do. If she were to die, presumably I would be to blame, since men should not be present at a birth, yet I clearly had to do something. I remembered what little medical knowledge I did possess and tried to assist. The baby was finally born and lived, as did the mother. The following day her mother came to visit me, with her sisters and other members of both the wife's and the husband's lineages, and talked for some time. One statement made was "now we know you are not a European, but a good person, and we are glad you are here as sister's son." The mother added that although she had wanted to call me earlier than she had, she had been frightened lest I pollute the homestead and endanger the birth; but she had been overcome by the argument that as I was not a Lugbara this could not apply to the situation. She had been wrong in that regard and yet paradoxically here was I, not a European, but a proper, trustworthy, person; being a "sister's son" helped, since sisters' sons could perform certain actions for someone that were too intimate to be done by a person's patrilineal kin. She was puzzled, realizing that her argument was, in the terms of her own culture, paradoxical. Until the previous day I had been a European, or at least more a European than a Lugbara; the scale had now tilted slightly and I could be regarded as more a Lugbara than a European.

Somewhat cynically one might well ask what is the point of discussing all this about the fieldworkers' changing role. The anthropologist is not undergoing a course in psychoanalysis, although the experience of being a field anthropologist may almost certainly be as intensive as being under analysis—it is not guided but in many respects remarkably similar (I write as someone who has not experienced analysis, so any indignant analyst can contentedly shoot me down here). The anthropologist is engaged in an arduous task of trying to understand and interpret a culture other than his own, and must retain this as being his only task for a period of two years. His behavior in the role he is given by his hosts is determined—or should be determined—by this single aim. Ultimately I am here leading to the question of how and when does one know that one has a reasonable idea of the culture and organization that one is studying. With this problem goes another that is present throughout one's field research and that is implicit in all that I have written so far: this is how does one estimate the accuracy, relevance, and completeness of the information given by informants. Clearly there are times when one is deliberately misled but it is much more common for one to be given incomplete information through no bad intention or fault of informants. The criterion for knowing that one has understood a culture and the cultural behavior that one witnesses might be said to be that one can predict what is likely to be the answer given to questions about them. The word predict here raises many epistomological questions that cannot be discussed in a book of this size; but something should be said of them since it seems to me that they are important. One cannot predict human behavior in the way that an astronomer can predict the appearance of a comet. The Lugbara cannot do that for their own behavior nor we for ours. However, it is not so much a matter of prediction of the future as of understanding the completeness and complementarity of the set of roles played before one in a given social situation. For example, the sacrificial rites that I have mentioned earlier were dramas played out for a certain end, with the actors being those taking part, the dead ancestors, Divine Spirit, and myself. Perhaps it would be better to call them scenes in a long drawn out drama than individual dramas themselves: none could fully be understood in isolation from the others. Each of these scenes had an expected number of actors whose roles were in a certain pattern of relationships and were composed of certain expected items of behavior. If one of these were missing or were misplayed the Lugbara would realize this and would state that the ritual concerned would be ineffective and should therefore be performed on another occasion. My competence at analysis of the situation was made clear only when I could myself realize that a particular role was missing, miscast, misplayed, or in some other way out of its proper place in the whole constellation of roles whose correct performance made up the scene before me.

I come here to an important point when one is studying nontraditional or innovative social behavior. When the prophets and the Christian evangelists initiated their ritual performances in response to situations of radical conflict, ambiguity, and change, the response to them by ordinary Lugbara was precisely that of bewilderment, uncertainty, irritation, and even anger because they could not comprehend a total and expected pattern in the scene before them. It was only at the very end of my stay that I was able to interpret in this way the Lugbara reaction to such figures and to realize that I did in fact understand something of Lugbara ritual performances. The same applied of course to many other situations, such as the behavior of many administrators and missionaries to that of many "New People" and, of course, to my own behavior. I first noticed this when I heard some Lugbara telling other Lugbara of the events that had occurred when several of us had visited southern Uganda. Their description of what we had seen and done were couched in terms that were very different from my own and which I saw at first as a distortion of our experiences. During that visit we had been to one or two Lugbara settlements of labor migrants, and the men with me could not place properly the behavior of those migrants because the scenes they were playing were as it were part of a different drama to that with which they were familiar in their homeland. It was after this that I began what I found to be extremely fruitful discussions in which I compared the accounts given to me by close informants of events and situations that we together had witnessed to my own description of the same events and situations that I had written down immediately on my return from them. The more I learned about Lugbara the closer were our various accounts of these same events, except on the few occasions when we had traveled into non-Lugbara situations, some of which I could interpret correctly by my own cultural traditions and others in which we were all ignorant of the expected dramatic structure of what we saw (such as a visit to the Kuku of the Sudan). In brief, what I am trying to say is that one cannot predict the events of a given situation but one can see the structure or pattern within the scene that is part of a total drama; and one then knows that one understands as much of another culture as one can hope to understand.

I had been warned by my teacher, Professor Evans-Pritchard, that there is a time when one thinks one is wasting one's time and is a failure. He was correct. In my case it was about nine months after I first entered Lugbaraland. I seemed to have no understanding of the language, I seemed to have no friends or confidants, I seemed to know nothing of the people or their culture. This sense of failure and of frustration would seem to affect us all sooner or later, I am told by colleagues. It was in my case compounded of several elements, most of them connected with my own somewhat romantic and optimistic expectations about my role among the Lugbara.

I had been trained to be a research anthropologist, and this stay among the Lugbara whom I wished to study was in a sense, as I saw it at that time, the culmination of a long period of apprenticeship: the apprentice, although hardly a master, was at least thrown on his own resources as a craftsman. I do not clearly remember exactly what I hoped to achieve even within a few months, but when very little seemed to have been achieved I felt lonely and despondent. I think that probably I had written too many initial field notes. My diary was another matter and when I look at it now I realize its value; but my first half-year's field notes are virtually useless except on a few matters such as technology, and these lack any sociological understanding.

I see also now how much of my sense of frustration, and much else of what I felt and did, were due to my own uncertainty as to my role among the Lugbara. It would be expected that one would have this sense of uncertainty during the period when one is being given a mature status by one's hosts: and indeed I experienced it at this precise time. It was clear to me, whether I liked always to admit it or not, that I was never completely accepted as one of themselves by the people among whom I worked—as I have mentioned before, a stranger can never be accepted, despite the self-deception of many sentimental travellers in Africa. I was always ultimately under the protection of the central government, whether they had wished to leave me alone or to deport me. The visitor longs to be accepted by his hosts, both emotionally and otherwise. I found for myself that there are likely to be three ways in which a fieldworker—or at least an anthropological fieldworker, whose position is very different from that of an economist, sociologist, teacher, historian, technician, or others—tries, consciously or not, to attain this affective link. I am assuming here, of course, that he is a fieldworker, that is, an objective observer; a full participant in the life of his hosts, even from his point of view if not from theirs, is no longer an observer in the anthropological sense. Perhaps this is both the easiest and emotionally the only satisfying course to take, but it makes research impossible and its findings unreliable. The three ways easily open to observer are to assist his hosts in such ways as providing them with medicine; to act as their spokesman vis-à-vis the central government or other external agency that his hosts find it difficult to deal with; and to build up a series of mutual friendship obligations that in some way fall short of complete participant equality. It is clear that these three courses (with full participation as the fourth) differ in the degree to which the fieldworker regards his hosts as objects. As Lévi-Strauss has written, one can only observe people as objects, whether we or they like it or not. But we are also people, and find the objective role as an emotionally unsatisfying one. One problem is obvious: that if we play the roles I have mentioned above, since they are all to one degree or other asymmetrical, they become frustrating. Probably the first response of most people is to accuse the other party of being selfish, or greedy, or in some other way showing that they lack the purity of one's own motives. If one gives several hours a week to dressing dirty and unsightly wounds and sores, one becomes annoyed when one's patients do not follow medical routine; if one gives a patient drugs one gets angry if he gives or sells them to others. If one puts in a word to the agent of the central government on behalf of people who are badly represented there, one may grow resentful if one's advice in the matter to the people one is representing is not taken, or if they try to presume on one's powers and demand more help than one can give while still retaining the role of impartial observer. If one has a friend—and I acquired a handful of close friends about whose behavior I could not remain impartial or objective—one expects him not to abuse that friendship, even if the abuse is in our cultural terms and not in his.

I am not saying that one should not grow angry, resentful, or frustrated at these responses. I am saying merely that at times I did, and from conversations with anthropological colleagues I have found that they did the same. I am saying merely that the role of the anthropological fieldworker is one of paradox, ambiguity, and uncertainty, and these are increased with the greater degree of difference in cultural expectations between his hosts and himself. There is not much that one can do about his hosts' behavior, but there is quite a lot one can do about his own. In my view, the most important thing is to know exactly what is one's own role as an observer, however one's hosts may regard it or their own. As I have said at the beginning of this book, my teacher told me that the most important part of a fieldworker's abilities is to have good manners, since these imply a knowledge of one's own status and values in interpersonal relations. To have this knowledge is, of course, to avoid condescension and patronizing, faults that are found, I fear, most particularly among those fieldworkers who assume, for one reason or another, that they have some special innate sympathy for and intuitive understanding of the people among whom they are living. Most of these merely think that they have these desirable qualities and their behavior is usually, in my experience, one that generates ambiguity and misunderstanding. Let me give two trivial examples. Lugbara always insisted that I should behave as a "European," or rather as a European without power over them, although I behaved as a pleasant and powerless human being who happened to have been born "across Lake Albert." If I did not dress in a fairly formal and clean manner they did not approve, saying that I was behaving "like a Greek" (the nearest thing in their particular experience to a "poor white") and was regarding them as unworthy of respect and good manners.

And whenever I invited acquaintances to my hut to drink or to eat they expected at least some of the beer to be "European" and served in glasses and at least some of the food to be served on a plate and eaten with fork or spoon. No one likes a slummer, whether in New York or in the Appalachians: why should people in an African city or village be expected to be any different? I am not saying, of course, that the observer should behave like a caricature of an Anglo-Indian colonel: that is as far on the other side; and one could argue that that kind of behavior is due also to uncertainty and often to fear, especially one expressed in collective and ethnic terms.

I am saying that the role of the anthropological fieldworker is not an easy one, and that the chief difficulty is usually one that arises from the paradox in his role, that he must be both objective and yet be a participant to the greatest degree that he can while still retaining objectivity. This is not advice for people who must cope with neighbors, or teach them, or administer them or have any other kind of role. Others with somewhat similar difficulties, of which the most obvious is probably the psychoanalyst, meet them differently. But there is here an essential difference that the analyst is an objective observer only with regard to individuals for ritually defined periods, whereas the anthropologist has the far harder task of being unable and unwilling to set aside ritually defined interview periods. There are, as we all know, many anthropologists who have done precisely this: they set certain times aside for clearly defined interviews, and live outside the fieldwork situation at other times. Except in the case engaged in ethnological reconstruction, as among certain American Indian groups, for example, I cannot see the value of doing this. It is a denial of the role of fieldworker.

Writing Up the Field Material

Finally I should say something about the writing-up of the data I had collected on my return to England from Uganda. After all, a man who has spent two years or twenty years on ethnographic field research but does not write up his findings for public use might just as well never have been to the field as far as the discipline of anthropology is concerned. As we all know there are some anthropologists who find it virtually impossible to set down their findings on paper. I assume that they find the paradox of being an anthropological fieldworker so difficult that they cannot readjust to their own culture.

I found on my return to England considerable difficulty in leaving one culture for another, even though the second had been my own. My first recollection is of noticing various minutiae of behavior in England of which I had previously been unaware. For example, I noticed how English women—but not English men—looked quickly at one another's clothing in passing in the streets. Coming as I had done from a virtually naked people I could perhaps hardly fail to see the social significance placed on wearing the clothes suitable to one's social position and aspirations. Again I soon noticed how English women would appear ashamed of being pregnant, whereas among the Lugbara to be pregnant is a source of pride and a cause for congratulation by patting the woman's stomach—something that I only just stopped myself doing on more than one occasion in England. I noticed what seemed to me to be the loudness and ill-manners of the children although what of course I was really seeing was the difference between Lugbara culture, in which children know their status as incipient adults, and English culture in which children have a subculture and an indeterminate status. I think that all anthropologists have similar experiences when returning from the field. This sense of strangeness and of awareness did not last for more than a few weeks, but it made clear to me my sense of uncertainty as to my proper role of a person who had lived in more than one culture and tried to observe more than one set of social values.

Looking back to my behavior after my return I see now that my uncertainty as to my role was expressed, as it is in most cases, by an excitement and a garrulousness concerning the Lugbara, whom I discussed avidly with anyone whom I met and was willing to listen to me. They were "my people," the object of an intense personal experience which I was willing to interpret to others although not totally willing to share with them. My own sense of uncertainty was lessened by the fact that I returned to a department in which all members had themselves done fieldwork or were planning to do it, and many of whom had only just returned from the field. This latter group was in the eyes of its own members set apart, and there can be no doubt that the excitement and fascination we felt for our common work was both helpful to us in a psychological sense and fruitful for us with regard to thinking about and interpreting our field experience and material.

I had one academic year in which to write a doctoral dissertation on my fieldwork, and I had chosen for the title of my thesis the very general one of "The social organization of the Lugbara of Uganda," which could of course cover virtually anything. I was fortunate at having no work other than to write the dissertation, although I did also have the immediate obligation of writing a report on labor migration. I was told that the dissertation would act as my formal report to those institutions that had sponsored my fieldwork. I spent those nine months mainly in writing the dissertation, which involved presenting some of the material I had collected so as to give an orderly picture of the society. This was not quite so easy as it may sound, since the various notions as to pattern and structure that I had held in my mind at the end of my actual field period soon proved not to be fully adequate when I attempted to put them down on paper. When I could no longer see the wood for the trees I was lucky in being able to turn to my labor migration report, in which the trees themselves were of major importance. By writing up the material for the thesis I was being made to objectivize my experiences and thus to resolve again the paradox of the anthropologist that I have mentioned above. I need not go into details of the thesis itself, which is from my viewpoint today a very inadequate presentation of Lugbara society. I think that there is often far too much pressure placed upon younger anthropologists to have a doctoral dissertation published immediately as a hard-cover monograph. I would say that a thesis is one thing and a book is another; the former is something to be got rid of as soon as possible, whereas the latter is a much more important work which is the real *raison d'être* of one's being privileged to be an anthropologist at all. By the summer of 1953, therefore, I had written a report on labor migration for the Government of Uganda, and had submitted and had accepted the dissertation.

I was at this point extremely fortunate—more so than I realized at the time—to be able to return to Lugbaraland for a period of three months during the summer. I did this in the company of three other people, so I was able to finish my fieldwork among the Lugbara both while working with a team and also after I had had a long period of writing and thinking about the former material that I had collected. There is no need in discussing this work, since for my part I spent most of the time in filling in gaps of information that had become apparent to me during the time I was writing the dissertation. The people with me were three students, all of my own academic standing: one was a soil chemist, one a botanist, and the third a geographer. All were excellent at the work they did and between us we were able to collect a great deal of valuable data regarding Lugbara ecology and agriculture. I found that my style of work was hardly possible in the company of other people, since we were simply too many to be accepted easily by the Lugbara at any one time. We were able efficiently to measure fields and to discover details of ecology that I found extremely important and meaningful when added to my former information about such matters as patterns of settlement and processes of group segmentation. But it was not possible to set up the close personal ties that had been so important for me during my own previous work. One man may be accepted as a quasi-kinsman, but three more were too many. All I need say here is that if the four of us had gone to Lugbaraland in the way in which I had gone myself three years previously we could not have acquired any very close knowledge of the workings of Lugbara society. We might have been very efficient at collecting quantifiable data, but any close and intimate knowledge of Lugbara culture and its values would not have been possible for us to collect, due simply to the inhibiting factor of our being so many strangers that Lugbara could not easily have absorbed us as "kinsmen." I think that this would not hold true of a husband and wife team, for the simple reason that a husband and wife could easily be accepted into the kinship system. But this was not possible for four unrelated men and I do not think the Lugbara found it easy or possible to regard us as being in any sense brothers to one another, which might have resolved that particular problem. However, I shall not continue this particular discussion, because although we worked as a team our situation was unusual, in that one of us had already spent two years in the area. We were therefore not in the position of a newly arrived team and our particular experience is of little value to other people in a more usual situation.

What is worth saying about this final visit is that it was perhaps the most immediately productive of any three-month period I had spent there. First, because I knew at that time exactly what were the points that I was investigating, and that with my two-year former experience the very fact that I was forced by my company to behave somewhat distantly and objectively removed many of the personal difficulties as well as many of the personal delights of my main fieldwork tour. In later years I was able to do fieldwork in Zanzibar and in Nigeria, and much the same is true of those researches. I was in an objective sense a far more competent fieldworker, for the very reason that my tie with the people whom I was studying was much less emotionally laden than that I had had with the Lugbara. I was able on these later occasions not to put myself into the position of paradox that I had been in among the Lugbara. This was not merely because these were second and third field projects but also because they were shorter and directed to specific research projects: in Zanzibar the study of land tenure and in Lagos that of immigrant associations. I was able to control any sense of uncertainty and frustration to a far greater degree but my work was more superficial, more objective, and with much less understanding and less sympathy and affection. I was not involved in anything in the same sense as among the Lugbara. I do not mean to say that I could not have been if I had had longer and less clearly defined projects: I am merely reporting my own experience. But these several years later I do not remember the people of either Zanzibar or Lagos as I do the Lugbara.

Publications on the Lugbara

Looking back with the wisdom of hindsight I can see that I should have planned a program of publications immediately after finishing my doctoral dissertation. I can see that probably the best way of doing this is to publish articles on limited topics which can later, after comments and discussion on them with other people, become the main part of a full-length book. In addition, a short general account would have been very useful: I could have referred readers of articles to it for the ethnographic background. I admit, however, that my own plan of publication, if indeed it even merits such a term, has been very haphazard; I have written on various topics as I have happened to grow particularly interested in them—and this has meant that there are some aspects of Lugbara culture on which I have written nothing for the public ethnographic record. Here I shall not presume to present a complete bibliography of what I have published on the Lugbara, but shall list some of the more useful accounts, not in chronological order but by topic.

I have published one general monograph on the Lugbara, under the title *The Lugbara of Uganda* (Case Studies in Cultural Anthropology series, Holt, Rinehart and Winston, New York, 1965). Other publications may conveniently be divided into certain principal topics, which the reader may consult as he is interested:

Economics, Labor Migration, Trade

Labor migration among the Lugbara. London: Colonial Office, 1952.
"Land and population in West Nile District, Uganda" (with D. J. Greenland), *Geographical Journal* 120(4), December 1954:446–457.
"Trade and markets among the Lugbara of Uganda," pp. 561–578 in P. Bohannan and G. Dalton (eds.), *Markets in Africa*, Evanston, Ill.: Northwestern University Press, 1962.

Political System, Chiefship, and the Beginnings of Social Stratification

"The political system of the Lugbara of the Nile-Congo Divide," pp. 203–229 in J. Middleton and D. Tait (eds.), *Tribes without Rulers*, London: Routledge and Kegan Paul, 1958.

"The Lugbara," pp. 326–343 in A. I. Richards (ed.), *East African Chiefs*, London: Faber and Faber, 1960.

"The resolution of conflict among the Lugbara of Uganda," pp. 141–154 in M. Swartz, V. Turner, and A. Tuden (eds.), *Political Anthropology*, Chicago: Aldine Press, 1966.

"Conflict and variation in Lugbaraland," pp. 151–162 in M. Swartz (ed.), *Local-level politics*, Chicago: Aldine Press, 1968.

Religion, Cosmology, Magic, and Witchcraft

"Some social aspects of Lugbara myth," *Africa* 24(3), July 1954:189–199.

"The concept of 'bewitching' in Lugbara," *Africa* 25(3), July 1955:252–260.

"Myth, history, and mourning taboos in Lugbara," *Uganda Journal* 19(2), September 1955:194–203.

Lugbara religion: Ritual and Authority among an East African People. London: Oxford University Press for International African Institute, 1960.

"The social significance of Lugbara personal names," *Uganda Journal* 25(1), March 1961:34–42.

"Witchcraft and sorcery in Lugbara," pp. 257–275 in J. Middleton and E. Winter (eds.), *Witchcraft and Sorcery in East Africa*, London: Routledge and Kegan Paul, 1963.

"The Yakan or Allah Water Cult among the Lugbara," *Journal of the Royal Anthropological Institute* 93(1), 1963:80–108.

"Some categories of dual classification among the Lugbara of Uganda," *History of Religions* 7(3), February 1968:187–208.

"Oracles and divination among the Lugbara," pp. 261–277 in M. Douglas and P. Kaberry (eds.), *Man in Africa*, London: Tavistock Publications, 1969.

"Spirit possession among the Lugbara," pp. 220–231 in J. Beattie and J. Middleton (eds.), *Spirit Mediumship and Society in Africa*, London: Routledge and Kegan Paul, 1969.

Various other papers are in press at the present time, but the above will give the reader some notion of the kind of publications that have been made on the Lugbara. In addition, there is one article on the neighboring and culturally similar (although politically very different) Madi:

"Notes on the political organization of the Madi of Uganda," *African Studies* 14(1), March 1955:29–36.

5A XII.75

STUDIES IN
ANTHROPOLOGICAL METHOD

General Editors
GEORGE AND LOUISE SPINDLER
Stanford University